What Fatso Taught Me

What Fatso Taught Me

Lessons on Weight Loss and Overcoming Overeating

Eric Johnson

Writers Club Press
San Jose New York Lincoln Shanghai

What Fatso Taught Me
Lessons on Weight Loss and Overcoming Overeating

Writers Club Press
an imprint of iUniverse, Inc.

For information address:
iUniverse, Inc.
5220 S. 16th St., Suite 200
Lincoln, NE 68512
www.iuniverse.com

ISBN: 0-595-20503-8

Printed in the United States of America

*This book is dedicated to all the fat kids out there.
Whether you are 5, 10, 15, 25, 35 or older, it's time to move on.
You can be everything you dream to be.*

I would like to thank Mom and Jodi.

Also, Jeff, Karina, Chris, Greta, Rose, and Gail.

Contents

Thanks to Jan Lefebvre, for believing.

Introduction

On a recent outing to the grocery store, a caption on the cover of one of the latest women's mags caught my attention. "Is the needle on your scale stuck? We'll tell you how to get it moving down." As has been the case for the last 25 years of my life, whenever I see a fat-reducing promise, my adrenaline rises, my mood lifts, and feelings of hope surge. Even at 175 pounds, the promise of losing weight still has narcotic properties for me. I grabbed the magazine and started thumbing through it to find the article. You want to know what the article revealed? In a nutshell… eat less, exercise more, be sure to get protein at every meal, and perhaps settle for more realistic weight loss goals. Groundbreaking!

*   *   *

You see a lot of fat people these days… *a lot*. A confusing fact when you think of all the diets, eating plans, and philosophies of fat floating around. **I don't believe for one second that anyone is content with being fat.** Now don't get me wrong; many overweight folks have found a level of acceptance with themselves (thank God), but I would bet that any one of them would prefer being at their ideal weight and having a sane, happy, and unfettered relationship with food. You may be one of them.

I'm so sad when I see a fat person. I'm especially sad when I see all the fat men because society has overlooked their desires to be thin. As little boys we were praised for being big eaters. In addition, we were also taught to hide our feelings, to be strong and brave, to not give in to emotions, and to find our own way in the world. Overeating played into all of this. When you felt confused, scared or unsure, you ate because that was what good little boys did. When in doubt, get strength and comfort from food.

Women have it tough too. The female standard of beauty in our society is more closely linked to a skinny body than it is for men. Men can be big and still be perceived as strong and jovial. Women are just fat. And in the same way that little boys are encouraged to be big eaters, girls are subtly encouraged to begin dieting about the same time that they begin eating solid foods.

So, if all these diet and weight loss programs are around, why is everybody so fat? *I firmly believe that all the diets and weight loss programs are in a large part to blame for this fat epidemic.* Most of these plans not only kill any real, personal joy associated with food and eating, but they also make the overweight person believe that the answer to his or her weight problem is in someone or something else. The objective of many of these pills, drinks, and food-encounter groups is to get you hooked on them and caught in a continuous cycle of dependence. A little digging soon reveals that everything you need to know to lose weight is already inside of you, waiting to be unearthed.

I know how it feels to be fat. I was very fat the first 28 years of my life (with an all-time high of 380). I overate, avoided exercise, over-exercised, loaded up on fat-free carbos, threw up, dieted on cabbage soup, ate protein… you get the picture. I understand the facade you create so that people won't know how bad you really feel about yourself. I know well the self-loathing, the hating of your stomach or chest or arms or legs or butt. How you feel different from everyone else. The discomfort you feel after you've gorged. The constant hope that tomorrow will be the day it will all change. Putting your life and happiness on hold until you are thin. You look at the thin, fit folks at the lake or the gym, the men comfortable without their shirts and the women in their tank tops, and you wonder how they got so lucky.

*   *   *

Things can be different. Very different. For most of my life I was so caught up in unhealthy attitudes about myself and food, I didn't think I would ever climb out from under. At 380 it's hard to imagine yourself without a 52-inch waist…but I lost over 200 pounds. I would like my experiences to help you overcome your food and weight battles. Hopefully you will see yourself in my story. **The first thing to remember is that there is nothing wrong with you as you are. However, there is also nothing wrong with wanting to be thin.** Getting to the truth of why you eat so much, and do so even without wanting to, is the act of uncovering the person that you were put on this earth to be. It's time to find that person and move on.

Part I

Growing Up Fat...

Chapter 1

Born to be Fat?

When I was six years old I was nearly killed by a Dairy Queen vanilla malt. My mom, my sister and I (all of us hearty-sized) were wedged into a plastic booth at one of the new Brazier Dairy Queens in a suburb of Minneapolis, waiting for our skinny dad to bring us our DQ treats. Mine was a great big, creamy vanilla malt. After setting all the treats onto our table, Dad turned to get straws, spoons and lots of napkins. Never turn your back on a 100-pound six-year-old with food in front of him.

Anxious as a kid with a new toy, I flicked off the plastic lid, wrapped my little hands around the mammoth cup, and tipped it to my mouth. Seeing what was about to happen, my mom screamed, "Eric, no!" It was too late. The entire malt avalanched out of its cup and onto my face. I couldn't breathe and started gasping for air. It felt like my head was being held under ice-cold water.

Mom reached over the table and cleared my nose and mouth with her fingers as Dad started to wipe me off with his red bandana hankie. I resumed breathing...stunned, embarrassed, and bubbling up to cry.

There I sat: fat, exhausted from literally inhaling food, sad, and unfulfilled. That about sums up the next 20 or so years of my eating.

*   *   *

My mom began telling me at an early age that I was not born to be fat. Those words stuck with me—a glimmer of hope but also a source of confusion. I wanted to believe her so badly, but I wondered which kids were the ones who were born to be fat and if I wasn't supposed to be, why was I? Someone must *have* to be fat. Mom's reasoning was that I had never had a weight problem up until the time I was four. Actually, quite the opposite was true. I was skin and bones to the point that the doctor had expressed concern over my apparent lack of eating. I had been born with the longest fingers my mother had ever seen on a baby, and, even at my heaviest (380 on a really bad day when I was 19), I have always had very long, skinny, bony fingers and hands. I looked at them as a sign from God that my mom was right—I wasn't meant to be fat. So again I ask, "What the hell happened?"

I wasn't sexually molested as a child. I wasn't physically, verbally or emotionally abused either (at least by my parents). I grew up in a generally peaceful, loving household. My mother was funny and creative, and my dad was nurturing and calm. However, in a society soaked with 24-hour cable, internet, and TV news reports that constantly bombard us with stories of horrifying abuse and neglect of children, **those of us who grew up in a basically loving, two-parent household are sometimes hesitant to say out loud that we have some battle scars**. Confronting issues when you've had a basically normal, healthy upbringing feels self-indulgent. Yet, the silent sufferings can be the most damaging. No one promised us a perfect childhood, but we do have the right (and responsibility) to make peace with our past and move on to live the lives we were born to live.

The ultimate conclusion I make about my life-long battle with food and eating is that I was clearly making the conscious choice to put all that food in my mouth all those years. I was responsible for the way I looked, and I was getting something in return for all that eating…and whatever I was getting, at least at the time, was worth it to me. This is an important realization for anyone who overeats to make. **Not until you realize that you are not a helpless victim, a randomly chosen fat person, can you also accept that you have the capacity to stop eating so**

much. No regrets or self-blame are necessary. You were handling the events of your life in the best way you knew how.

*   *   *

Sensitive Tendencies

I remember at the age of four, sitting on a pile of straw in our barn with my sister, waiting for my dad to finish milking the cows. Milking cows was a hard job. It was cold, damp work. The majority of the time was spent bending over, not to mention dealing with cows, which are usually unpredictable beasts. My dad was no doubt and quite understandably edgy.

I had a flair for the dramatic, even at that age, and I was spouting off a series of high-pitched boo-hoos. I remember my dad barking a sharp "Eric" in an attempt to get me to shut up. That moment is as vivid to me today as when I was four. I was ashamed and embarrassed, my feelings made worse by my sister's giggles. I also remember feeling, even at the age of four, a sense of disapproval, that I had disappointed my dad and did not fit his ideal picture of what a son should be. All of this at the age of four!

My mom tells me I was a very colicky baby. My dad would walk the floors with me night after night. He was the only one who had the patience to handle a screaming baby hour after hour. I believe I was showing the early signs of sensitivity towards my environment, and, at that age, not even food could help me. As a parent, what do you do with a baby that won't shut up and won't eat? I guess you do your best and pray that one day it will be better. At least I was expressing how I felt and not censoring my feelings. When I was angry or hungry or hurt, I cried. I didn't stop to consider if I should cry, whether it would be proper or make someone feel bad. I cried a lot, but then I stopped. **We can learn a lot from babies about expressing ourselves.**

We lived on a farm about three miles outside of town, but it might as well have been 500 miles. My parents were hard workers. On top of farming 165 acres and milking 50 cows, my mom helped my grandma with her catering business… and feeding hungry Germans and Scandinavians is no easy job. My sister and I spent all of our time at home…no pre-school, no ballet, no early childhood development this and that, which was fine. However, given my natural tendency to be like a turtle (retracting into my shell), going to kindergarten for the first time was traumatic. I have only a few memories of my first year in school.

There wasn't enough room at the regular school for the kindergarten classes, so we were shuffled across the street to the social hall of the Methodist church. I remember I hatched a chick from an egg in an incubator and I knew what a kaleidoscope was when the teacher asked. To this day, my mom retells these memories with pride. It's a glorious feeling to make your parents proud. Shaming them is hell, especially when you've experienced the joy and pride-filled payoff for doing well. If you're a sensitive little kid and you feel even a little crappy about yourself, the look of pride in your parents' eyes when you've done a good thing begins to be something for which you strive. When you don't get it, it's like a little cut in the heart. **From a very early age the reactions of others may become a higher priority than your own thoughts and emotions.**

In kindergarten you are able to get away pretty well with being an introvert. Crying, pouting and peeing in your pants are still pretty standard fare. I remember crying over the stresses of spilled milk and hearing one of the other kidlets (Allan Melbourne, who later in life tragically ran his girlfriend down on a country road) say, "It's Eric again!" I also remember going to the bathroom, which was always a trauma for me (public bathrooms can be such brutal places), and sinking into a little cubbyhole by the door, terrified to go back out and face all the other kids. I was five! What kind of pressure was I imposing on myself? I remember thinking that I was supposed to be feeling something that I wasn't feeling—joy or excitement over playing and being with the other kids, but I just wasn't. **I began to put on a little mask of how I thought I should act.**

When visitors would come to our house, I would hide behind the couch. I have to hand it to myself for displaying flashes of such honest emotions. I remember my parents (God bless them) never scolded me or made me come out. They just let me stay behind the couch. When the aunts and uncles asked where Eric was, they simply told them that I was behind the couch and that I would be out later. What a tribute to my parents. They may not have always known how to handle a highly sensitive kid, but they had a very fundamental respect for me as well as my differences, and they expected it from others. I think they were loners themselves and envied that I was young and could get away with it—they had a cartoon that hung in our kitchen that read, "The trouble with being a farmer is you are always home when people visit."

Sunday School was also a trauma. Mom had to sit with me while all the children gathered in the church basement before being lead to different rooms according to age. She would then shadow me to my classroom and sit on one of the miniature chairs by the door as the other little kids and I gathered around a table to learn that Jesus loved us if we were good. I still hold a vivid memory of my poor mother: beehive hairdo, wrapped in her beige car coat with faux-mink collar, cocked halfway on the mini-chair. I'm sure she was dying of a mix of embarrassment and boredom, but I felt warm, safe, and happy with her there. When she came along with me, I loved Sunday school. When she didn't, I was scared to death.

Some of us come into this world with a natural inclination towards sensitivity. It is not being oversensitive. It is merely a tendency towards sensitivity to external stimuli. It's difficult to go through life with this inclination. Everything is so much more harsh and raw. Criticism is more acute, a scolding goes deeper, and rejection is a death sentence. Now, on the other hand, joy is heightened, happiness is usually closer to ecstasy, and love has narcotic properties to it. But a heightened sensitivity leaves you bare to the world, and if that goes unrecognized by those around you (and yourself), especially at an early age, you must latch on to some sort of coping mechanism to get through it, to soften the blows. I latched onto food and eating. I think that is why so many artists and performers fight battles with addiction; sensitivity towards the outside world is requisite to making art.

This natural inclination towards sensitivity that some of us have is the only explanation I can come up with as to why some people leave childhood with emotional bruises and others don't. Most likely if you hold battle scars from growing up, it was because you were sensitive or open and receptive to the stimuli around you (parents beliefs, remarks from your peers) and did not feel you had the right to feel the way you really felt or speak your own truth. *There is no such thing as a wrong feeling. Listening to and honoring your feelings is telling the truth.* Remember, you are not responsible for determining the correct way to respond to or act towards someone else. By responding to a person in the manner we think he or she wants us to respond is the art of making other people's decisions for them. Not only is it not our place to do this, but we also rob ourselves of our own heart, mind, and spirit when we do this. It is your responsibility to start honoring your own heart and responding to others accordingly.

Sensitivity is not a bad thing. It is not a character flaw requiring counseling to lessen or eliminate. The more sensitive a person you are, the better you are at putting yourself in another person's position. Insensitive people, on the other hand, are a pain in the behind. They go through life unaware of those around them and, in the end, rob themselves of real relationships and all the wonders and miracles that everyday life offers. They make annoying co-workers, hurtful partners, and distant family members. Sensitive folks, on the other hand, make great collaborators, great listeners, and fun, spontaneous life companions.

When it comes to tactics in handling your own sensitivity (and in living your life to its fullest and truest sense), *The Four Agreements* by Don Miguel Ruiz offers great wisdom. Mr. Ruiz lays out four agreements to make with yourself and live by. In a nutshell, the agreements are to be impeccable with your word, to not make assumptions, to always do your best (but no more), and to not take anything personally. If you allow yourself to focus on the last thought in partic-ular, you may soon notice a wash of calm come over you.

In addition to saving us unnecessary misery, Mr. Ruiz reminds us that we cannot take anything personally because the way that people respond to us has everything to do with who *they* are and how they feel about *themselves* and little to do with who *we* are. What a relief this is. And what peace and security it brings to us to be ourselves.

When we take what others do or say personally, we accept it as truth, and we are in a sense, as Mr. Ruiz puts it, poisoned by them. Committing ourselves to not taking anything personally, opens us up to live with a new sense of freedom to be happy and live our lives as we see fit. *The Four Agreements* is a profound book that pretty much sums up the art of happy, meaningful living in 100 pages or so. Check it out.

*   *   *

Good Little Eaters

Our society praises big eating in little boys. Little boys who are big eaters are good little boys. They're just like Daddy, and they are going to grow into little football players. This is an especially disappointing message to receive if you don't want to be a football player. My cousin Kyle was a big eater and a little football player. I, on the other hand, was just fat. I kept on eating because it received a positive response in my family. I was expected to eat a lot and to like it. At least I knew I could do that much right.

You have to understand the kind of food lineage from which I come. Food reigns as not only love, but also as the family jewels, particularly on my mother's side of the family. Grandma Myrtle was famous in Gaylord, Minnesota for her food. She was a round, proud 250-pounder with the class and carriage of the First Lady. She had purchased with husband Ed, the Sibley Hotel of Gaylord, Minnesota. Previously owned by her parents (her mother Minnie was also a big girl), it was a rambling old structure with a big kitchen in its belly. Over the years, after operating the hotel and serving Midwestern fare in its dining room, the Sibley Hotel morphed into Sibley House Catering, a sort of Southern Minnesota food icon in the 1970's and 80's. Trust me; ask someone in Sibley County about Sibley House Catering and they will talk about the yummy food. I still stumble upon people to this day who grew up in the area and know of my grandma. I also ran into one person who, without fully realizing who I was, referred to Grandma as "this giant woman who just sat in this big, empty building and cooked food all the time."

My mother continued the food tradition and is a wonderful cook. The downside while growing up was the central role that food played in my life. ***It became a learned response to not only eat when I was confused, stressed or sad, but also when I was happy or content. Any heightened emotion called for eating.*** The upside was that when I finally learned to love food enough to have it in my life in healthy and joyous quantities, I had developed a pretty vast knowledge and appreciation of it.

Now, you probably know all too well that you do not have to be exposed to great food to develop an addiction to it. Junk food (usually anything in a crunchy cellophane package and neon orange) is even more accessible. We had plenty of that around as well. The interesting thing about junk food is that most of us deny that it really is food, so we inhale it, and it's gone before we know we've eaten it or certainly enjoyed it.

As a society, we begin the pattern of praising eating in children (both boys and girls) early in life. I hear myself do it with my niece. "Big babies are healthy babies" rings around the house of a newborn. When I baby-sat for my niece, I always figured that if she ate, she wasn't sick and must be happy. I would take this one step further, and if I found myself confused as to how to handle her behavior, I would try to get her to eat. It was a sure sign everything was okay if she did and at least I would feel better. Now, I certainly understand that a baby who doesn't want to eat for long periods of time may most definitely have a medical problem, but I often see food used as a pacifier for babies, and any deviation from abundant eating is viewed with concern. No thanks to me, but quite luckily, my niece, now five, has developed into a young girl with eating habits I envy. She eats only what she likes, when she likes. She prefers some healthy foods to unhealthy ones, and she is very active. Also, she is very good at saying how she feels and stating what she needs.

*   *   *

So where does that leave us?

Some kids are just different. I think all kids are different in some way; after all, what is normal? However, some of our differences stick out like sore thumbs. Shyness, a longing to be at home alone, sensitivity, and a need to be with your mother are not differences that receive a lot of positive reinforcement in our world, or at least in Arlington, Minnesota. I think we quickly become so afraid of someone or something different in our society. What appears to be different in a child is stopped and fixed in attempts to get the little person back on track. *What happens is when we stop or try to fix a different but generally safe and healthy kid, at some level that kid gets stuck at that age and spends the rest of his or her life trying to make sense of the feelings that were tagged as wrong.* The kid continues to act out these emotions, often with a rebellious bent, to prove to himself and the world that there is nothing wrong with him.

My parents were wonderful and giving. Even with these two on my side, most likely because of my propensity towards sensitivity and my large size, I got the message from an early age that I was separate and different from everyone else. Because of this feeling of being separate, I began to see the world as unreliable and, consequently, scary. I just didn't ever feel that everything was going to be okay. *If you don't believe that everything is going to be okay, you start developing tactics in an attempt to make everything okay or at least protect yourself from distress. You hide your feelings, you become a good little kid, and you behave the way you think you should. Food relieves the pressures you put on yourself.* When you couple this with religious training that God is somewhere out there, and only if you are good enough, pray hard enough or are somehow deserving will you get what you want, this message solidifies in your psyche. A lot to carry around as a little kid. Food is a great place to turn. It's immediate gratification; always on hand, always reliable, pleasurable, fun, and, as a little kid in our society, you're encouraged to eat it.

*   *   *

A Letter to the World from a Five-Year-Old Little Fat Boy

Dear World,

Am I bad? Is everything going to be okay? I know I'm different, but leave me alone, let me be me, and love me for who I am. Don't worry about me. I just have different things to offer. Spend time with me, doing what I love to do. I like to draw. Buy me markers and paper and draw with me. I like to sing. Take me to music class, even if I'm a boy, and sing with me. I like to build. Build things for me and with me. I like to plant things. Grow a garden with me.

Little Fat Kid

*   *   *

Now, the secret to the above letter is this: If you didn't get the nurturing you needed while growing up, it is your responsibility to give it to yourself now. Recover something that you lost as a child because you were different or fat. Maybe it was a sport you loved or painting or camping. What made you stop doing it? Did you have a bad experience that made you think you didn't deserve to do it or you didn't deserve to have fun? Did no one recognize your love for it, nurture it or encourage you? A sure sign of abandoned passions are feelings of jealousy when you see someone doing something you feel you could do, but aren't. If you are jealous of people on stage or in a movie, jealous of people who exercise or jealous of your friend who paints, it's helpful to think about why you are jealous.

You're an adult now, and you have the capacity to do or have anything you wish, if it is something you truly need. Make a list of ten things that you loved to do as a kid. Don't censor yourself. If it doesn't sound like anything lofty, that's okay. It can be as simple as chewing gum or whittling birds out of wood. Look at your list and pick one or two things you would really like to have back in your life.

When I was seven I loved drawing houses and designing elaborate fountains and gardens in front of them. I don't know why I ever stopped. I've begun doing that again, and when I do my mind and heart soar. It's like I'm creating, by myself, my own little part of the world. Go claim what is yours.

Once again, if you believe that you were born with a tendency towards sensitivity to external stimulus, stop looking at it as a fault or liability. There is no such thing as being oversensitive; you simply possess your own personal level of sensitivity to the world. It probably makes you a wonderful friend and an insightful, creative person. Instead of denying and second-guessing your feelings, listen to them. They are your intuition trying to tell you something.

It is time to stop putting your sense of self in the hands of others. This is when sensitivity becomes a problem. When another person's look or comment is all we have to base our sense of self on, we are left with nothing. Begin listening to your own heart rather than the random thoughts of others. Stop and do it right now, in the present moment. Become very still, breathe deeply, and focus on your heart. You may begin to be aware of a warm, glowing sensation. This is where you need to go to in times of confusion or craziness. Listen to what comes to you when you focus on your heart rather than the words of others. You will not go wrong. As the German poet and play-wright Goethe wrote, *"Just trust yourself; then you will know how to live."*

Chapter 2

The 3 R's: Readin', Ritin' and Rejection

It seems to me that the ideal education would include learning the basics (reading, writing and arithmetic) while at the same time discovering (and accepting and appreciating) more about yourself. We are *all* so full of potential. Sometimes I drive down the street and just look at people, especially the visually downtrodden, and I want to yell, "You can be anything you want to be!" It's easy to see it in others; isn't it? ***Where do we get off track from expecting the best for ourselves?***

I'm not sure if grade school is easier or more difficult in a small town, but in my hometown if you weren't armed and dangerous when going off to school, you were a sitting duck. Even sadder, armed and dangerous meant being as much like everyone else as you could possibly be. I sense that most schools are like this.

My teachers in elementary school were a collection of German warhorses (my hometown was an equal mix of hard-edged Germans and passive Scandinavians). Most often, they took the pound-it-in rather than charm-it-out approach to teaching. I don't blame them. I really don't. I'm sure they were dictated by what they were expected to teach by the end of their assigned grade level, in addition to all the usual pressures of life. ***However, the bottom line about learning is that if you're not being appreciated or at least understood as an individual, all the other stuff you're expected to learn just seems to be pointless.***

Learning can only take place in a safe environment. You compound all this with being very fat and…ouch.

When I was in second grade, Mom came home from parent/teacher conferences with a report that some of the teachers were concerned about my size, particularly in phy. ed. where I would breathe heavily and sweat profusely. I remember the phy. ed. teacher, Mrs. Wally—half jail warden, half wicked witch. She looked like she herself had flunked phy. ed. Thick and plow-horseish, she had a fortress of black hair and a face like a big clock. Once when I was cowering in the back during an aggressive game of trench ball, she came over and asked me what I was doing in the back. I gave some mousy answer, scared to death of her. She pushed me into the game so hard that I tripped and fell. **_Isn't phy. ed. supposed to be healthy?_**

The teachers in my small hometown (population 2,000 in a good year) didn't know how to handle a little fat boy, especially one who was quiet and shy. To them (and I think it's the German lineage that does this) fat people were jolly and gutsy. I think these tanks were fundamentally sad sorts, their sizes indicated this, but they couldn't stop the war of life long enough to figure this out. You stop aggressing, and you get hit. Small towns really can be war zones.

*   *   *

Being Called Fatso

Sadly, you get used to being called fatso in school. It's actually a rather cool name. If it weren't for what it meant, I actually wouldn't have minded being called it. I always felt that if other kids just got to know me, they'd love me, but when someone sums you up in one cruel word, you pretty much figure, "What's the use?". It was never the kids in my own class that would call me it; they had gotten used to the sight of a 100-pound kid. It always happened when our class walked by another class. A "fatso" was inevitable. I got to the point that I felt great if it just stayed to a minimum, say once or twice a day. Talk about aspiring to success.

There were other fat kids in school who seemed to be able to escape the slings of misfortune's arrows or at least they seemed to have the means to not take it so personally. They probably were the less sensitive type talked about earlier. Or maybe I possessed unique characteristics that made be stand out even more, but each "fatso" was a mortal wound to me. I took each one as a stamp of disapproval, and if you get enough of that you start to give up even the things you love.

*   *   *

Little Fat Kids Are Easy Targets

In Mrs. Anderville's third grade class, we were divided up by what reading group we were in (advanced, middle or remedial). Consequently, all the kids thought of the room as being divided up by the smart kids, the average kids, the dummies, and then the mildly retarded. **Labels, labels and more labels prevailed.** I was actually in the advanced reading group, but somehow I always felt like I was in it by mistake. Someone must have goofed-up on a test score or the teachers felt sorry for me because I was fat.

I can honestly say without flinching that Mrs. Anderville did not like me. However, she loved and favored (to the point of reinventing the term teacher's pet) Julie Hayman. Julie was thin, beautiful, and smart. Not to mention, she was the daughter of a "big shot," as my mother would say. Her dad owned Hayman's Clothing Store, a small town Marshall Fields wannabe.

In third grade you learn the multiplication tables. Dull, but I guess necessary. Julie memorized better than anyone, and Mrs. Anderville loved it. Memorizing was neat and clean and orderly. You either did it or you didn't, and Julie was quick when we did the flash cards.

I hold a crystal clear memory of one test day. There was this unspoken, but very present competition to see who could be the first or one of the first to turn in a test paper. In a need to prove myself in some way, I raced through the test, scribbling down numbers madly while barely looking at the math problems, hoping to turn it in before Julie, which I did. I expected to just get the paper back the next day with a low or mediocre score, but Mrs. Anderville had other plans. She ripped into me in front of the class. I remember the real stinger was, "It's a shame that you don't even know what one plus one is." Ouch. No taking me aside to see what was up with my test paper. No genuine concern over my performance. No understanding of how I was already ashamed to just be me and needed no further humiliation. Just a chance to get at the little fat boy. What frustrates me the most when I look back at the experience is that I just sat there, dumbstruck, like I had been slapped in the face. I could have at least said, "It's two."

I behaved similarly when all the boys in the class were forced to write 100 times "I will not misbehave in the bathroom." I never went into the bathroom on the group bathroom outings. I was too shy to pee in front of others, and I was always sure I would be humiliated in some way. *Not thinking you have the right to pee sets up some very unhealthy body issues in a kid.* I would always wait outside the bathroom for everyone to finish, and Mrs. Anderville knew that, but when all the other boys in the class got in trouble for peeing on each other and participating in other water sports, she punished me as well. We all had to do our writing at home, and I recall being too embarrassed to let Mom and Dad see what I was doing (thinking they would be disappointed in me). When they finally asked me what I was frantically scribbling, I told them, but I added that I shouldn't have to do it because I wasn't involved. Much to their credit, they made me stop and tell Mrs. Anderville the next day that I wasn't in the bathroom. I did as they told, and she gave in.

Now I can't say for certain that she disliked me because I was fat, but I do know that that's what I felt at the time, and I have always had good instincts. I also know one of her daughters suffered from anorexia in her high school years, so I can't help but surmise that she had some weight issues swimming around in her head as well.

Mrs. Anderville was not responsible for my being shy and intro-verted. She was not responsible for my being fat. She was not respon-sible for weight issues that I had later on in my life and that I continue to battle with, but she does represent a fundamental mind set that does exist in our world towards little fat kids. **Little fat kids are easy targets for abuse, especially little fat boys, because they are trained to put up with whatever abuse comes their way.** It goes back to society's image of the good little eater and the little football player. Little fat boys, because of their physical appearance, assume the persona of adult men—stoic, solid and emotionally tempered. However, inside they may be crying for help.

Little fat kids are often viewed as self indulgent, messy little pleas-ure-seekers who are too lazy to do the work required to be thin. Many people, children and adults alike, can't get past this idea. Overeating is a choice, but it represents so many other issues going on in the little one's life, real issues that deserve attention.

I ask all of you adults out there to look a bit deeper at these little fat kids and try to find out what is going on. You may have to press a bit more and be a little more persistent. **These little kids have learned to put up walls and hide their feelings as a coping mechanism.** They are certainly not going to ask for help. Please, make the effort.

*   *   *

My First Diet

The summer between fourth and fifth grade, I went on my first diet. I was ecstatic. I felt bad about being fat and could never quite under-stand why I had to be that way. I had entertained ridiculous theories as to why I was fat. It was because I didn't pick up my toys. It was because I ate boogers. It was because I didn't pray at night. I had plans in place such as doing the ridiculous calisthenics routine we learned in phy. ed. every day during summer vacation or not eating for three months straight.

But this summer our entire family was going on a diet. We would be a normal family, and I would be like all the other kids. Dad wasn't really overweight, maybe ten pounds, but he was going to join us. At first there was talk about all four of us going to Weight Watchers, which I thought was just the coolest thing ever, but one day the plan switched to cooking and eating as dictated by the *Better Homes and Gardens Calorie Counters Cookbook*. I think the whole family trekking off to Weight Watchers every week was just a little too exposing, especially in a catty little town. Weight Watchers in the 70's wasn't like it is now. From what I remember, rumors of being weighed in front of the entire room and taping pictures of pigs in your window if you gained weight circled the town.

Whenever we talked as a family about losing weight and getting thin, my main comment was always how exciting it would be to not be made fun of or be called "fatso" anymore. **Mom always made sure to tell me that we never have control over what others say. It was her way of telling me to get strength from within.**

At the start of the diet summer I was 165 pounds. Favorite recipes from the plan were ham slices with a ring of pineapple, open-faced broiled hamburgers with a thick slice of onion, and Rye-Crisp pizzas. The Rye Crisp pizza was the greatest because it tasted like a normal pizza, but it was on a Rye-Crisp, and it was "diet." I do remember that for a couple of weeks I never cheated, not even a bit, and we did stick with the eating regime for the bulk of the summer. I worshipped daily at the altar of the scale, but couldn't get below the 150 mark, still a lot for a ten-year-old. After the first couple of weeks, I was sneaking too much food, in addition to not getting any kind of exercise on a consistent basis. Basically I sat around all day, watched television, and waited to lose weight. My parents (God bless them) believed that my sister and I should have relaxing summers, so we never had to work much around the farm or house. I remember that I had interests like drawing, music and gardening, but I never allowed myself to do them very much. I remember feeling that the things I liked to do were so different from the people around me, that doing them only made me feel more different. How sad. If I could have fought that feeling and become immersed in the things I loved, I would have probably spent less time in the kitchen and less time obsessing about eating. Instead, I ate and watched TV…very easy and very accessible.

My parents had the best of intentions, but *I think the most that came out of the diet summer was an obsession with the scale and weighing myself and a notion in my head of the negative power of food.* Our little bible, *The Better Homes and Gardens Calorie Counters Cookbook*, was going to make my life better, but it didn't.

School came around, and the diet went away. I have to admit that if I had been my parents, I wouldn't have known what to do with my eating either. There was a definite obsession with food in my house, and I had adopted that as a way of life as well (more than anyone else in the family). I was clearly eating too much and not exercising, but how does the cycle get broken?

*   *   *

Too Busy to Do Anything but Eat

My parents worked a lot and very hard. As farmers, their workday started at 5 a.m. and ended, hopefully, by 8 p.m. When they weren't milking the cows, they were cleaning the barn or feeding the calves or fixing the automatic barn cleaner or meeting with the veterinarian or—you get the idea. In the warm months, they had to do all this on top of planting the fields, cultivating (or weeding), harvesting, baling hay, fixing the machinery when it broke down and so on. On Saturdays, my mom would work for my grandma and her catering business. Breakfast was a hurried affair during the week, toast and milk if there was no time and the school bus was coming down the road (God forbid we would have to run to catch it). Dinner (served at noon, when we were home) was the sanest meal. At least we would all sit down. Supper (in the evening) was snacking whenever the milking would be done, usually on cheese and crackers or whatever you could find in the fridge. I was usually sneaking to the house several times during the evening milking to grab a few mouthfuls, so I'm sure I ended up having about five crappy suppers.

My point from all of this is **where was my parents' joy? When did they have fun?** When did they have time to do what they loved? All they ever did was work. Without going into great detail, both of them had worked like dogs from a very early age—Dad from the age of 15 when he took over the family farm after his parents died and Mom from about the same age when her family bought the Sibley Hotel. **Food is a relatively cheap and very accessible form of fun and entertainment. It's also a pretty effective and acceptable drug.** Eating was the chief form of joy in our household, and I can't say for sure about the rest of my family, but it was eating me up.

I don't blame my parents one bit. Contemporary fat theorists might have suggested that we all go for a walk at the end of the day and then go eat a meal that was a perfect reflection of the food pyramid. But my parents were exhausted. What I believe was really at fault is whatever belief system put them in the mindset that they had to work non-stop and never look deeply at what they needed to be happy. If I could go back and do anything, it would be to change that.

*   *   *

I Can Eat A Whole Pizza

By the next summer I seemed to have settled into a "if you can't beat 'em, join 'em" approach. **Feeling betrayed by the world of dieting, I decided to be a little "big man" and fit in by being a big eater.** Somehow I picked up the idea that eating a whole pizza was a sign of being grown up, and one night when I was left alone to fend for myself for supper, I took on the challenge and won. I didn't enjoy it. I felt stuffed, but I bragged about it when my parents came home. I knew that they would be proud of me, and in some strange way I felt accepted and closer to the rest of the family.

In sixth grade, we were weighed at the beginning and the end of the year, for what purpose I do not know. If there had been any purpose to it, I would have hoped someone would have taken some action over a 168-pound eleven-year-old. Did this not seem to be a problem to anyone? *Overeating (or undereating) is a telltale sign of childhood depression, but I don't think there was anyone in my school who could recognize this or was willing to take the time to care.* A few teachers had such weight issues of their own that to aggressively pursue the subject with a child might have required the difficult task of admitting they had some skeletons in their own closets.

I think it also speaks of the passive Scandinavian, stay-out-of-other-people's-business atmosphere that prevailed in the area. To voice a concern would be to risk creating conflict, and that was a mortal sin. It was better to just let it go and hope that it corrected itself over time. *Plus, there's a part of me that believes there was mindset present that it's good to keep a scapegoat in the school.* Keep someone down at all times so that you feel better about yourself. It's distracting and keeps the pressure off of everyone else to be perfect.

The semiyearly weigh-in began a life-long pattern of using weight loss as a tool of approval. If I could just lose and get to a normal weight by the end of the year weigh-in, everyone would like me, not give me raised eyebrows as the arm of the scale went up, and everything would be okay. I gained 18 pounds during sixth grade, ending at 186. Mary Beseke lost 16 (by eating grapefruit for breakfast and taco salad for lunch, she said), but I gained 18.

*   *   *

Dear Whomever Is Out There,

Hello! Does it seem fine to you that I'm nine years old and 170 pounds? It's not. Please help me! I want to be like everyone else so bad that I just pretend I'm fine in hopes that my fat will go away. I'm sad when people call me "fatso" and make fun of me. I'm scared to death about going into junior high, and I hate wearing chopped-off pants from the men's department. I was so embarrassed when the sales lady gave me a dirty look and shook her head like I was disgusting. Why are you ignoring me when I need help? I'm the kid, and you're the adult. Maybe we could eat good foods and exercise together. Can't you see that I'm too scared to ask for help?

Little Fat Kid

*   *   *

It's time to take care of yourself like you were hoping to be taken care of when you were a little fat kid. Don't ignore yourself the way you were once ignored. I think about how much easier my life would have been if I had asked for help at that time in my life and lost weight. Give yourself the attention you have been asking for all along.

Healthy eating and taking care of yourself is the one thing you have the final say over. No one can take it away from you. **When you feel like the things you want in life aren't coming to you, focus on the things you have immediate control over, like healthy eating and exercising, and all you desire and truly need will come your way.**

Chapter 3

Junior High: 12 Years and 200 Pounds Later

Any weaknesses or insecurities of a kid become a giant bull's-eye on the chest when he or she enters puberty and junior high. It must be the combination of raging hormones and raging insecurities, but everyone becomes either the attacker or the attacked. It was confusing to me why I suddenly became the target of cruelty and what seemed like hate and was certainly abuse. I didn't think I had changed at all. Why had everyone else? I was instantly even more of an outsider. Food and eating became not only my best friend, but also my only friend.

The majority of the onslaught occurred in phy. ed. Once again, I thought phy. ed. was supposed to be healthy. The humiliation would begin in the showers. Stripping naked in front of thirty other boys when you're the odd man out, a miniature Pillsbury doughboy, is tantamount to war torture to a twelve-year-old. I think I was the fattest to come through the school in quite some time, so I was a little like a side show freak. Once they got done looking at me in awe, they started laughing and pointing, then pushing, slapping and hitting. I was so quiet and shy, I certainly couldn't fight back, and, if I had, it would have been thirty against one. Matters didn't get any better out on the athletic field. I couldn't run, I couldn't throw, and I couldn't catch—criminal offenses in that crowd.

Being an outsider in the locker room pretty much establishes you as a complete loser everywhere else in the school. Your days are filled with anticipating the next punch in the arm or kick to the back of the knee. Walking the halls was like walking a street in a bad neighborhood—constant surveillance to see who your next attacker might be. When I got to the classroom, I would strategize to keep away from the mean boys as best I could. Sometimes I couldn't, and I would have to sit through class with the taunting comments behind me. There was a Bully Hall of Fame that ran like a pack of dogs and, at least in my mind, seemed to be in existence to make my life hell.

Even though it's tough to do, it's vital to forgive in order to heal and move on. They were just kids; some were probably living at home the hell I was living at school. If I am to accept that I didn't have the wherewithal at the time to ask, beg or plead for help, I need to grant them the same. Until you forgive the mistakes of others, you are basically telling yourself that they were right. Forgiveness is a powerful tool.

*   *   *

Weighing In

The twice-yearly weigh-in in phy. ed. was the pinnacle of humiliation. Not only would I be paraded up to the scale, like a pig going to slaughter, but Mr. Kildhim, the phy. ed. teacher/athletic director/bus driver/driver's ed. teacher, would revel in announcing my weight to the entire room. "2-4-0." It was like when we would sell cows and listen for the weight and price to be announced on the radio. The reactions were the same as when people see the enormous hog at the State Fair swine barn: an odd mix of shock, excitement, and disgust.

Could Mr. Kildhim have recognized I had a problem or at least acknowledged how scared I was and weighed me in private like in sixth grade? After all, he was the phy. ed. teacher. Hello! Phy. ed. is short for physical education. I think he had a theory that if he made it public enough I would be shamed into doing something about it. Also, we were all guys, and in Arlington that meant you were all supposed to be the same…no reason to hide anything. If you were different, that was wrong, and they'd get you to be the same. Probably the saddest part was I grew to want to be more like those creatures that taunted me. At least then I wouldn't stick out so much.

All day I heard "fatso" shouted at me, accompanied by cruel laughter and wicked sneers. I wandered around our farm at night, sick with worry over what I had to endure during the day. I tried God, I read articles wherever I could find them, I searched for solutions like smiling at everyone or looking straight ahead like a zombie. Once I tried drinking some Lysol, not to kill myself, but to perhaps make me sick enough to call attention to the problem. I also contemplated jumping out of the barn to break my leg. In retrospect, this wouldn't have been such a bad plan.

I was definitely suffering from some kind of depression. I kept eating more and more to try to numb the pain. I was faking sickness at least once a week and I was getting very bad grades. I had no interest in anything except eating and zoning out in front of the TV.

*   *   *

Lesson to Learn: Ask for Help

There was a part of me that would not allow myself to ask for help. I think this is very common in boys and men. It goes along with the maxim that men will never ask for directions. We have a genetically programmed need to figure things out for ourselves. To go along with that is a survival instinct to ignore conflict. I see it in many of my male friends. You take this and add a Midwestern Lutheran setting of swallowing your feelings, and you've got a little kid who is in a lot of pain and doesn't know how to ask for help… and he's surrounded by people who find it easier not to ask.

Once my sister said to me in front of Mom that a friend of hers had asked why I always hung out with girls and didn't have any guy friends. I was so embarrassed that I turned ten shades of red and responded as if her friend were crazy. Mom later came to me and asked if I had any guy friends. I was too embarrassed to say no, and I didn't want my parents to worry about me. Also, I think I had developed the impression that I was so separate and different that there really wasn't anything to be done to help. There was no way that anyone who came into contact with me could give me what I needed to fit in.

Growing up, I taught myself to bottle up my feelings, wants, and needs... to label them as silly, selfish or too demanding. These bottled up emotions manifested themselves in more ways than just my eating. I chewed on everything I could get my hands on: pens, my sleeves, and plastic toys...to name a few. My sister once fell and cut open her knee on a plastic baseball bat I had chewed to a gnarled mess. Not only were all the corners of our pillows chewed to threads, but all the arms of the chairs and couches (the ones I hid behind) were gnawed to bare wood. It was like having a puppy in the house.

I had also been a fairly good student in grade school, in spite of Mrs. Anderville's attempts, but my grades were continuing to slip badly. I couldn't concentrate when I was in school, and I was too upset at night to keep up on my homework. I slumped around the house at night, downtrodden and depressed. Food numbed this feeling, and when I ate I didn't think about what was going on at school. It was similar to how I've heard abused children speak of counting while they are getting hit. If you focus on the counting, you don't feel the pain.

I was also lagging in school because I was missing so much of it. In contemporary workplace language, I was taking mental health days. I would fake sickness, usually starting at six or so in the morning, but sometimes, using my talents for drama, beginning the night before. My parents were concerned about all the school I was missing, and they weren't stupid. They knew I wasn't sick. As a matter of fact, I never got sick, and this made me mad. Maybe it was all the vitamins I was getting from the surplus of food. Mom and Dad obviously could see I needed days off to deal with the stress, and they gave them to me. It was their way of helping at the time.

Thanks should also go to some teachers who tried to help in small ways. Mr. Hislip was a gentle, soft-spoken English and reading teacher. One day he knelt beside my desk and told me he thought I was a very sharp young man, but I wasn't progressing like the rest of the class, and he wondered if something was wrong. I should have said, "Yes. Everything is wrong. Please help me." But I didn't. I was too embarrassed about what was going on, and to open up to him first would have been betraying my parents—the male ego at work already. Thank you, Mr. Hislip, for trying.

Another gem, Mrs. Bouldher, the earth science teacher crossed with Auntie Mame, also gave a try. One afternoon while I was making up a test I had missed (a common occurrence), she gently questioned me on how I was doing and what I ate and gave soft suggestions as to what I perhaps should eat. I listened but crumbled inside at the idea of making myself vulnerable enough to ask for more help or take what she was saying seriously. We really do have to be ready for the help in order for it to do any good. *My eating was the only real comfort I allowed myself at the time.*

Letting your grades slip is serious business. A bad grade is not damaging if it is the best you can do, but performing below your potential, not doing your homework, and not knowing what's going on in class because you've missed so much school or you've been daydreaming is very damaging. You can always tell someone who has either been told that they're stupid or has surmised it from the events of their life (grades, teacher's comments, not knowing the answer). First of all, they tend to be people pleasers, desperately trying to hide their inner feelings of stupidity by getting people to like them. They also get very uncomfortable when asked their opinions or thoughts, in constant fear of being told they're wrong. Also, they easily give up their stand on an issue, also in fear of it being wrong. Coincidentally, these are also signs of an individual who has learned to see the world as a judgmental place where you may or may not get what you need. If you have a tendency towards sensitivity, this is all made worse.

Moral of the story: Ask for help. Recognize that everyone is different and that we all require differing means of getting through life. Offer help or inquire into whether help is needed when you see someone in trouble. Reminding yourself not to take things personally helps here. There should be no fear of feeling stupid for not knowing the answer.

*   *   *

The Biggest Kid in the School Didn't Eat Lunch

I understand that the teen years are tough for everyone, but they need not be unbearable. By the time I was a teenager, my eating was even more out of control. This was confusing because I knew I was eating too much, always feeling uncomfortable, but all the other guys my age seemed to be eating a lot too but didn't seem to be getting as huge as me, nor did they seem to be as miserable. I wouldn't eat breakfast because I would get up too late. I was so sad, I would lie in bed until the last possible second to make the bus. I wouldn't eat lunch either. I was too scared of facing everyone in the lunchroom (or lynchroom as I called it), so I just hung out by my locker during lunch hour. The biggest kid in the school didn't eat lunch. Interesting.

When I got home after school I would make up for it by eating ten meals: peanut butter sandwiches, leftovers, desserts, crackers and cheese, baloney, Cool Whip and whatever I could get my hands on, always washed down with several Diet Pepsis. If I had play practice after school, I would arrive home in time for dinner and eat about ten dinners. I wonder what kind of impact I was having on the grocery bill. I would return to the kitchen throughout the course of the night and clean up any leftovers and then start again on the sandwiches, the cookies, and whatever I could find. Once I couldn't find anything but raw bacon, so I ate it. *I was miserable but most of all feeling helpless and hopeless. These are sad, yet vague emotions; eating gave them some kind of definition. At least I had something to feel bad about...my disgusting overeating.* I would eat like a pig to hide my true feelings of rejection by my peers and the embarrassment over the situation, and then I would have clearly-defined emotions...disgust over what I had eaten and hatred of myself for being so weak.

Maybe the saddest part of it all was the fact that I loved (and do to this day) food, and I don't think I really enjoyed a single bite of it the whole time I was growing up. It held too many bad associations for me, and my daily thoughts of dieting mainly consisted of eliminating food from my life. Every day I punished myself, shaming myself for being such a disgusting pig, who was weak and lazy. Every day I vowed that I would prove to myself that I could deny myself food, get my act together, and get skinny. *It wasn't until much later that I acknowledged what a glorious thing food was, that I wanted it in my life and that I not only needed it for survival but deserved to have it. It was then that I made peace with it and lost weight.*

Every day I would vow to myself that tomorrow would be different. I admire my optimism at the time. There was a teenage boy in the clothing section of the JC Penney catalog who I worshipped. He was normal-sized, blonde and freckled, bedazzling in normal sized jeans and a t-shirt with no boobs. He was perfect, and I aspired to be him. I was aspiring to be a one-dimensional picture. I didn't care what he was like; he could have been dull, mean or even stupid, and I wouldn't have cared. If I could be him, everything would be perfect. I never got to be him; I only ate more and more and grew bigger and bigger.

When I look back at this time of my life, with 20 or so years of perspective, I would say that I was choosing to remain fat. *Remaining fat and feeling helpless was easier. It seemed to be the prouder approach and an alternative to saying that I had problems, needed help, my classmates hated me and made fun of me, and I was miserable and hated myself as a result.* Also, whatever thoughts were swimming around in my head that might chip away at my self-esteem could be nipped at the bud with my self-loathing thoughts about my size and my eating.

*   *   *

Is There A Purpose to the Hell of Junior High?

If there is a purpose to the hell of the junior high years, it is to learn how much you are like the other kids around you. No matter what our likes, dislikes, similarities or differences are, we all need to know that we are fundamentally the same. At this age, you've broken away from your family to an extent (hopefully), and **you look to the kids around you as a reflection of what is happening to you and as models of what the world expects of you. This builds a fundamental self-confidence; you are getting the message that you are okay, that there is nothing wrong with you. You feel safe in who you are.** This is the basis from which you discover and explore all the unique qualities about yourself.

Fat kids never get to fully realize this stage. You feel different, you are treated different, and you keep eating to quiet your restless feelings. You never receive that all-important signal that you are okay just as you are. So many little fat kids get caught in a life-long struggle to fit in and please those around them, sacrificing the next vital stage of discovering themselves.

*   *   *

A Letter to Anyone Who Can Help

Dear Anyone,

I don't know what's wrong with me. Nobody likes me or appreciates me. I don't feel like I fit in with anyone. Everyone thinks I'm weird... and so do I. My fat only makes me more of an outsider. I don't want to be this size anymore, and I want your help to lose weight and get some control over my life. Please help me. Tell me I'm normal. Help me not care what others are saying about me. ***Tell me I'm okay and it will be okay. Help me get healthy.*** I will run 10 miles a day and do yoga 30 minutes a day and read a health related book every week. Would that be fair? I'm sorry I don't have the guts or whatever it takes to make this change on my own, but I'm just a kid who's been beaten down by the bullies in my class. Half the time I don't even want to be alive. This isn't how life should be.

Little Fat Boy

Is anything on hold because you need help? Do you ask for help when you need it, or do you just put the blame on someone or something else when something doesn't come to you? You may need help getting started with your weight loss goals. Admitting you need help is the first step. Asking for it is the second. The help could be as simple as disclosing to a friend that you have weight loss dreams and need support.

*   *   *

A Note on "Phy. Ed."

What is the idea behind high school phy. ed. anyway? In most other classes, the attempt is at least made to teach fundamental skills that will either last a lifetime or set you up to continue the learning process. However, phy. ed. often seems to be just an excuse to get kids to run around like maniacs for an hour and burn off some adrenaline. American health (physical and mental) is in a state of crisis. Just walk down the street and see the number of overweight people. I recently saw on TV that 65% of Americans are obese (at least 20% over their recommended weight). Wouldn't high school phy. ed. be the perfect setting to educate kids on lifelong healthy choices?

Did we learn weight training? I remember spending a couple days on the weight machine, basically just going through the class one by one and seeing who could bench-press the most. Mr. Kildhim would check how strong we were without helping us or at least showing us how to become stronger.

Did we learn stretching exercises to prevent injury? No. We would just dive feet first into whatever activity we were doing. It could be why my knees are shot. How about healthy eating choices or stress management or setting fitness goals or incorporating health and physical fitness into a life-long process?

In all fairness, I've been told that many of these things are now being taught in at least the larger school phy. ed. classes. But I know there are still schools out there like Arlington in the 80's, and for those kids, I am sorry. Anyone who suffered through Marine-like phy. ed. classes and has since turned to discovering healthy life habits knows what I'm talking about.

Chapter 4

Senior High: Staring in the Face of 300 Pounds

As I went from junior high to high school, I seemed to be getting more different and everyone else seemed to be getting more the same. This shouldn't be a bad thing, but if you don't have the self-esteem in place to trust and accept your own changes, you grow to hate your differences rather than embrace them. I went through a period when I was dyeing my hair blonde. I think I was trying to be a different person.

I also yearned to start dressing with some flair and sense of personal style (as do most teenagers), but this is tough when you're shopping at Pamida (two steps down from Wal*Mart) and looking for 48-inch jeans. I ended up having about two pairs of pants and three shirts throughout high school. I remember catching a girl in my class, who was also hefty, pointing and commenting on my enormous khaki pants that I wore every other day. What was I supposed to do? There weren't a lot of choices for the big boys. I think that's why I dressed in wild prints in college after I left my hometown and lost some weight.

High school should be the time when you start finding your way in the world. Ideally speaking, we would enter these years feeling safe and loved, with enough in common with those around us to feel comfortable enough in our own skin to discover our talents and passions. *If you are still stuck in the "finding your place in the pack" stage of junior high, you will either alienate yourself by finding external ways of fitting in with the crowd or you will check out. Eating is a great way of checking out.* When you stuff food in your mouth you don't feel the pain, disappointment, and rejection. Furthermore, when you become fat you are actually putting yourself in control. You've come to see the world as a disappointing place, but by adding layers of fat you are able to say, "I'm not getting what I want or need out of life because I'm fat. If I take off the weight, which I may do someday, things will change."

*   *   *

Surrounding Myself with Food

I worked for my grandma's catering company from the time I was a freshman in high school until I was a sophomore in college. I wanted to work for her so bad that I would have done it for free. I had a calling to be with the food. It wasn't my conscious reason, but I think subconsciously, I wanted to be with it, and not just in an obsessive-compulsive way. Even then, on some level, I realized the magical, creative powers of food.

Every time I worked I would start out being a really good boy, vowing not to eat anything, but as the day wore on, I would begin to slip. The workers began the day by cutting and chopping radishes, celery, and carrot sticks for the relish trays. I loved the mix of red, orange and green. If I snuck a piece or two, it was no big deal. We would then go on to cut up the fresh fruit (watermelons, cantaloupe, honeydew) plus wash the grapes. If I took some of this, it was still no big deal. We would then load the vans to go off to wherever the wedding or event was. Once we arrived at the community hall or American Legion Club, I would begin sneaking food, and soon all hell would break loose.

My grandma and her "right hands" didn't care if you snuck food; they actually seemed to like it, like it was the ultimate form of flattery. I was an enormous high schooler during my catering years (around

280 by then), and during the early years, I also looked and sounded like a girl. I would get terribly nervous when the guests began to arrive because many of them would point and laugh at me. The kinder would just snicker or roll their eyes. My job was to help keep the buffet table filled with food. There were usually four lines going through at a time, so I had to hustle to keep the gravy bowls filled and the meat platters heaped. I would sweat a lot, especially on my head (I get this from my mother), and I think it kind of grossed out people to have me handling the food. Sometimes I would be running so hard and fast that I would get chest pains. I would chafe between my legs as a result of slipping jeans and sweaty thighs. After the madness of feeding 500 people, the workers all sat down to eat, and I would stuff myself. Sweaty and sore, I killed the pain with mountains of mashed potatoes, dressing (baked soggy bread), and thick turkey sandwiches. Why didn't I know about the Atkins diet? I was surrounded by protein.

Grandma's buffets typically included: roast turkey, ham, ham balls (a ham meatball), roast chicken (oven fried, really), occasionally roast beef (a pricier choice), dressing, corn, mashed potatoes and gravy, overnight fruit salad, coleslaw, rolls, relishes, pickles, cake and ice cream—you get the idea. My mother worked with my grandma from her twenties through her fifties. I remember five-gallon pails of beef stroganoff in the refrigerator for dinner. **Food seemed to be a metaphor in the family: I think of it as a heavy coat, a coat that you wear continuously. It doesn't entirely smother you, but it wears you down enough so that you are tired and can't see your true self.**

I hated high school so much that I think the catering business (which was in the neighboring town of Gaylord) was an escape for me. I think back to those days and wonder why I couldn't have been cultivating some of my own interests at home. My parents didn't make me work for Grandma; quite the opposite, I begged to. I was miserable from all the food, fat, and people making fun of me, but I was running towards the very thing that was making it worse. Why didn't someone do something, like a fat intervention?

My grandma's catering business and the kinds of food it served, the amounts and the frantic pace that surrounded the serving of it, represents a fundamental attitude towards food and eating that's common in the Midwest. Most often, no one talks. Many just shovel in the food, bodies hunched over and heads sunk down. There is a specific way that some people in the Midwest hold their shoveling-in fork. Most eaters hold a fork like a pencil, but many Midwesterners hold it with the handle hidden in the palm and the index finger resting near the tines. This allows for a quicker feeding. To many, food is not to be savored or celebrated, but rather it is to be inhaled without tasting.

My family, however, did recognize the wondrous aspects of food. My grandma and mother knew every cooking technique there was and have prepared some of the finest recipes I've ever experienced: Beef Burgundy, Lobster Thermidor, Beef with Horseradish, lovely green, enormous salads, exotic vegetable dishes, and elaborate desserts. Both women knew how to make the most of food. They were insightful and creative enough to raise cooking to an art form. Somehow, however, none of us (until much later) learned to control our eating. I think in my grandma's case, she had abandoned all her other life interests for food.

My grandma had class and was a very talented woman. We had an old photo of her hanging in our upstairs hallway as I was growing up. In the photo Grandma looked like a stately, beautiful, self-confident china doll. Her father, from what I hear, was a millionaire at one point in his life, but he lost it all in the stock market. He must have regained some of his wealth because when he sent my grandma off to Mankato State Teacher's College (now Minnesota State University-Mankato), he gave her a checkbook to write checks as she needed. I also hear that she studied the violin at McPhail School of Music in Minneapolis. How this fit into growing up in Gaylord, I'll never know, but I do know her sons still talk about it to this day with pride. She sewed like a tailor and gardened with skill and passion. Her crocheted projects were little museum pieces, expertly crafted with a nimble hand. She read nonfiction voraciously, was an expert on politics, and spoke and wrote with confidence, clarity, and wisdom. She had finesse in all areas of her life, but she was a good 100 to 150 pounds overweight her entire life. In the days that I knew her, her attentions were pretty much just focused on the food.

I loved my grandma, and I know she loved me. I could just tell. She died of congestive heart failure at the age of 89—not necessarily a fat person's disease, but I remember she was huge when she was lying in the hospital. Her final years were spent living in a trailer that my parents added on to the house as a makeshift mother-in-law's apartment. The final night that she was at home before going into the hospital for the last time, we made brown beef stew. It was her favorite. We all thought everything would be okay if she could eat a little—but she couldn't. Silently gathered around her kitchen table, I stuffed myself, Mother worried, and Grandma stared out the kitchen window.

*   *   *

Sex and Fat

Fat keeps a person from sex, or at least healthy sex. I was having no sex, but there was a fat girl in my class who was rumored to be quite popular with a neighboring town's football team. This was probably worse than having no sex. I always say, at least fat saved me from the sexually transmitted diseases of the sexual revolution.

Worse than missing out on the actual humpety-bumpety is the denial of any sexuality in your life. **Fat alienates you from any awareness or connection to your body, especially as a teenager. It's this very disconnect that keeps a lot of teens and adults fat. If you are being made fun of as a result of your fatness or feel overly self-conscious about your body, you will separate your mental self (psyche) from your physical self to maintain some semblance of self-esteem.** It's this separation of the mental, emotional, and spiritual self that snowballs and keeps you fat. You start to think of this fat body as something else and something you hate because it's making your life miserable. It gets you laughed at and is denying you fun and opportunities in life. Because you hate it, you punish it with overeating and, in some cases, anorexia and bulimia.

Healthy sex is a pleasurable act done out of love for yourself and another—a difficult concept for an overweight teen. Healthy sexuality is a necessary stage in development and helps a person define who they are and how they fit into the world. A lot has been written about our society's ideal of beauty. In a man it is a flat, washboard stomach, slim hips, bulging calves and a well-developed chest, arms, and back. Anything less is considered to be cause for concern, but a fat boy with boobs that many girls would envy and a tummy Santa certainly would can hardly take off his clothes in a locker room, not to mention get naked with someone for whom he has romantic feelings.

I do not want this to come off as if I'm condoning or encouraging teenage sex. If you are a teenager (under 18) reading this, please note, you are too young to be having sex. But I strongly feel that denying or shrouding feelings of sexuality (simply put, feeling sexually unattractive) is detrimental to your social and mental development. Fat does this to a person. *Even without losing weight, we need to accept ourselves as we are and begin accepting ourselves as attractive. Thinking you are attractive is 80% of appearing attractive.*

*   *   *

Richard Simmons: My Weight-Loss Fairy

At 16, I became obsessed with Richard Simmons. It was almost a love affair with the frantic, afro-headed god of the obese. I even drew a portrait of him in my art class. There were, of course, all the messages of loving yourself as you are and the hopes of getting thin that he preached, but I think, most of all, he represented someone who was very different but somehow managed to channel it into a successful and accepted existence.

Richard had a TV show that aired every day at 9 a.m. I watched it religiously during the summer and all too frequently during the school year when I would fake sickness. He had a motivational segment, a cooking segment, and an exercise segment (all in half an hour). I sat in the big overstuffed chair in our living room and watched the half hour of fantasy. Never did I get up to exercise or takes notes or even really try to introduce any of the ideas into my consciousness. Richard's preaching was a far away dream, which survived only in a little box with an antenna that pumped in other people's lives from far away.

I bought his book with $20 my grandma gave me for Christmas. I read it from cover to cover, but more like it was a romance novel than a self-help book. All the ideas sounded good, but I just couldn't fathom working them into my life. Not having a crutch to turn to in times of stress scared the hell out of me, and the thought of exercising my nearly 300 pound body exhausted me. Although Richard's book contained the information needed for me to lose weight, it didn't address the reason I was eating so much. This I wouldn't figure out until later.

Years later, when I was 26 and about 250 pounds, I went to see Richard Simmons live at the Eden Prairie Shopping Center. He was on a book promotion tour, and I gathered with 500 or so other fatties to see our cult hero in person. He put on a sort of cross between an Anthony Robbins motivational seminar and a rock concert. For his segment geared towards men, he pulled me out of the audience with five other moderately overweight men (accountant and banker types) and had us dance suggestively to stripper music. He gathered us in a huddle and told us in a feigned persona to "imagine 500 horny women out in the audience." We were to take turns dancing solo, our pelvises thrusting and testosterone leaking. The one who received the loudest applause would win $100. I was so mortified I barely moved, even though I knew I could boogie with the best. Probably because I had such high expectations, Richard came off as a fake to me. After the 45-minute program, the fattest of the fat were put at the front of

the autograph line. After ten minutes of videotaping Richard expressing the ultimate in concern, the cameras shut off and so did Richard.
He left; I mall-walked for an hour and went home. I had such idyllic
expectations for Richard that there was no way he could have lived up
to them.

Richard Simmons has the best interest of the overweight at heart.
The unconditional love he sends out to the morbidly, even terminally
obese is inspiring and humbling. Because his affection is so conta-
gious, I honestly think many of his fat followers don't move forward
in their own lives and with their own weight loss aspirations because
they are so hooked on the love he gives them, perhaps the first love
they have ever felt in their lives. They are looking to him for the
answers to their weight problems, rather than looking inside themselves. All the wheel-a-meals, powder drinks and grapefruit in the
world won't help until you focus on your reason for eating so much.
The saying "It's not what you eat; it's what's eating you" is pretty
much dead on. When you're a teen, I think you need help finding this
out. I was in my twenties before I did.

*   *   *

Letter from a Teenager to Anyone Who Will Help

Dear Someone,

I know I'm old enough to get my act together and lose weight
on my own. I just need some encouragement from those of
you who love me. Don't be afraid to talk about my fat. It may
be a shock at first, but I won't think you don't love me.
Actually, I'll know you love me even more because you are
taking an interest in me and letting me know you care. Losing
weight is scary, and, right now, it seems impossible. I need
your help. Please help me.

Please tell me you love me and that everything is going to be okay because I don't believe it will be. I feel like I have done something wrong and my life is miserable because I have been bad. I'm lonely, and I hate myself. I feel like a freak. I want to be happy, but I need help. I guess I expected more out of life. Sometimes I wish I were dead.

Bigger Little Fat Boy

*   *   *

Think of your supposed oddities and perceived weaknesses as strengths. There is more than one way to do anything. If you can't seem to fit in with a certain crowd, accept it as a blessing and a sign. It no doubt means that you would never realize your true self amongst those particular folks. If you are fired because you are not able to work in a particular fashion, multi-tasking for example, celebrate that you are able to focus thoroughly on a single project. If office politics drive you crazy, you could be a perfect candidate for self-employment. If you are a walker and have tried running but can't make the leap, take heart. Walking is a fabulous workout and less stressful on your joints. Trusting the validity of your own, sometimes-unusual self is the key, but it is sometimes difficult to remember to follow your own heart. (More on this later!)

Chapter 5

Moving Away from Home

As much as I hated high school and living in Arlington, I was terrified of leaving after I graduated from high school. I wanted to be done with high school and move on to other things, but I had no self-confidence and no real sense of what I wanted to do with my life. Not to mention, I loved my family. I was going off to college, and I was scared to death.

I was silly enough to think that I would get skinny just by going off to college. I envisioned myself keeping constantly busy with classes, studying, and play rehearsal (I wanted to be a Theatre major). Plus, I figured that without a kitchen and fully stocked fridge and pantry to sneak down to and raid, the fat would melt off. *I thought I could just leave all my past fears and insecurities by moving, but I soon discovered "wherever you go, there you are."* Well, during the fall of my freshman year I whizzed past the "freshman 15" and topped out at my all-time high of 380. When I left for school in August, nervous and insecure, I weighed 320. I gained 60 pounds in four months! I didn't even know that was possible. Of course I had Hardees, McDonalds and Domino's Pizza to thank for the help. The location changed, but my addiction to food hadn't, and instead of Mom's kitchen, I had an entire city at my disposal for my eating binges.

Change is difficult for everyone. I was moving away from home and my family for the first time, moving in with a total stranger, forced to make friends for the first time, and taking college classes. In my hometown I had gone to school in the same building with the same kids for all twelve years. I hated a lot of them, but there was a certain safety in not having to make new friends. At college, every time I met someone I felt that they quickly dismissed me because I was so huge. On my first day of college when my parents came with me, my dad, God bless him, told me how thin he thought I looked and that I really had taken off weight. I had gained 30 pounds over the summer, so he was clearly trying to buy me some confidence, but the gesture was appreciated.

*   *   *

Fighting With My Feelings

Bethany College was a tiny, private Lutheran college in Mankato, Minnesota. One night during the orientation weekend, all the students were corralled into the gymnasium to do painful icebreakers. The ones when you just had to talk were misery enough, but when we were instructed to sit on the knees of the person next to us to form a sort of human chain, I cracked and ran out of the gym. Thank God I had a car. I sped off to the nearest Hardees. I shoveled in my favorite: A Big Deluxe Combo with an enormous box of fries and, of course, a Diet Coke. I never went into the fast food places. I would drive through, which would allow me to just go on to the next place, collecting bags of wrappers in the back seat. I felt continually more miserable as I stuffed in the mounds of grease and salt, but I was numbed. I didn't have to think about getting along with all those perfect-looking kids in my strange, new world. I could just eat and bloat.

In retrospect, I wish I could have just let myself experience what I was feeling without torturing myself. There is nothing wrong with not wanting to sit on people's laps, in the best of circumstances. Needless to say, I ran out of the gym because I couldn't bear the thought of sitting on a stranger's lap when I weighed well over 300 pounds. Also, I was so self-conscious about my size that just being around strangers was painful. However, since college is about discovery, I wish I could have taken the experience as a sign to discover myself. I didn't need to get to know others better. ***I needed to get to know myself.*** But I had it in my head that I needed to do what I thought I was supposed to do, and that was, at least at the moment, to bond with my new classmates.

At the time, the conflict of the confusion was too much so I did the only thing I knew to do to help confusing, conflicting feelings go away—eat lots. In retrospect, I could have left calmly and gone for a walk. A movie would have also been a great alternative. I could have just not gone in the first place. I wish I had started keeping a journal at this point in my life. Finding a quiet place to write would have helped me greatly. But I wasn't yet ready to step back, take care of myself, and think about why I ate so much. It would be a while before I was ready for that. I think it's interesting to note that I chose a college that was really just like my high school—small with few people with whom I felt I had anything in common. It was as if I was trying to make sense of how uncomfortable I felt in high school by putting myself in a place where I could try again to fit in with my peers.

The fast food frenzies continued throughout the fall of my freshman year. I would drive from Hardees to McDonalds to Wendy's and then to the Holiday station for a few candy bars, whichever were four for a buck. Talk about driving under the influence! Halfway through the Hardees feast, I would feel a calm wash over me, my eyes would glaze, and my reactions would dull. I should have been arrested for being drunk behind the wheel. These runs would usually happen at about nine p.m., after I was done with play rehearsal or had studied a little or watched TV. And this was on top of three starchy cafeteria meals. I was also known as the guy in the dorm who would always go in on a pizza. They came from all the floors to search me out. It wasn't because I wanted the pizza. I hated eating in front of others. I did it so they would like me. Most of them would eat their half of the pizza and then leave. They would return only when they wanted to order again and couldn't find anyone else. I remember one night I went in on three different pizzas. I guess it's not too hard to see how I got to 380.

*   *   *

Hitting Rock Bottom

I had been big my whole life, but during Christmas break of my freshman year I caught a glimpse of my reflection in the window of the Benetton store at the mall. I literally turned around and walked by three more times, not believing what I saw. I didn't recognize myself. My head looked like a little softball on my huge, overgrown body, and my feet pointed to the side as I walked, like a penguin. When I arrived home I plowed through the snow to the barn to weigh myself (I had to weigh myself on an old feed scale). I stripped down to my undies, as I always did to get the lowest possible number, even though it was 10 degrees outside. I stepped on the platform and slid the marker north until the arm balanced at, oh my God, 380. My heart skipped. I was scared and amazed. I don't think I ate anything for the rest of the day.

I had grown huge. In all seriousness, I looked like a whiter, lumpier version of the Michelin man. No muscles, just lumps and rolls of soft, dimply fat. My rear end was the biggest part of me (like two pillows), followed by my stuffed sausage thighs and then my stomach. I wore an enormous pair of sweatpants most of the time. My chest looked like it belonged on a woman, and I had a chin that went to the top of my chest. My eyes were red and puffy, probably from so much salt, and, sadly enough, my face was in a permanent state of smile from years of trying to get people to like me.

You hear stories of people hitting rock bottom before they can come back. This was rock bottom for me. It would take me a while to come all the way back and tackle all of the issues around my eating, but I'm relieved to say that from this point forward I slowly began to lose weight. I never weighed 380 again. Maybe I needed to reach a point where there was no ignoring or second-guessing that there was a problem. Small changes here and there were what got my weight moving in a downward motion. In a sense, I was scared straight.

Now, the upside of weighing in at 380 is you don't have to do much to lose a few pounds. As a matter of fact, I barely ate anything for two days and lost almost ten pounds. The bigger you are, the faster it falls. It was Christmas time. I was surrounded by reindeer cookies, roasted goose, and eggnog, so I imbibed until the New Year with a plan to do whatever it took to get down to a normal weight. I would start when I returned to school for the new semester.

*   *   *

Small Changes

I didn't have any solid reasons in place in my head for losing weight, no thoughts of how unhealthy I was or that I couldn't walk up a single flight of stairs without sweating. I wasn't even thinking about how the weight was putting so many issues on hold... sex, asserting myself, and gaining self-esteem. I only had the number in place, and that was okay for the time being. **Sometimes you have to have a little success to breed more success.** I needed to prove to myself that I could lose weight, make positive changes, and see some of these changes in the mirror. If I could just drop some poundage, I would clarify my goals later.

I made small, yet surprisingly effective changes throughout the rest of the year at school. I wouldn't go on my fast food frenzies anymore, partly with weigh loss in mind but also because I was continually making more friends, and I stayed in at night to hang out and study with them. It's interesting to note that when I stayed in, I made the friends. I guess I was too busy with my love affair with food prior to this point to make friends. Pizza deliveries dwindled to once a week at the most. I was no longer the pizza booty call.

A friend, Eddy Soul, took me along on his afternoon workouts. We would run around the soccer field, me taking enormous breaks when I thought my heart would explode, and then we would go off to the weight room to lift. I really wasn't much interested in the exercise. I was more interested in having a friend to spend time with who seemed to genuinely like me. Little did he know, I was in love with him. Motivation takes all forms.

Another good friend, Kevin Fost, would tell me how he could see I was losing weight, that I would be the best looking guy if I lost weight, and to keep it up. Wasn't it Mark Twain who said something like, "I can survive two weeks off a compliment."?

Walking was just beginning to be acknowledged as a viable form of exercise. It seemed easy enough to do… no panting, no ache in the knees, no chest pains, and as beneficial as running. When the weather warmed up, I started walking forty-five minutes or so a day. I did it in hopes of losing more weight. As I walked, I imagined my enormous butt getting smaller, as if the motion of the walking was melting the fat away, it was dripping down my legs, and I was depositing it on the sidewalk, leaving it behind me. Disgusting, but the creative visualization seemed to work. It was also great therapy. **There was a commercial running during the 90's that said something like "If there were more walkers, there would be fewer psychiatrists."** I couldn't agree more. It cleared my head and allowed me to think through all the crazy thoughts from the day, which seemed to unempower them. I would end each walk with positive thoughts, part endorphins being released, part visualization of my big butt getting smaller, and part deliberate, positive self-talk. I sing the powers of walking to this day.

By summertime I was inching down towards 300, still a long road ahead, but enough of a loss to garner comments from almost everyone who cared enough to say anything. It was time to move back home for the summer. I was excited to be home again, but I soon learned that change, good or bad, is a hard thing for me. I think it is for everyone with self-esteem issues. **One needs to have tactics in place to weather change, but I hadn't arrived at that stage yet.** Instead of having a firm basis is my own psyche and solid sense of self-worth to maintain some sense of constancy during periods of change, I was subject to whatever influences were around me. Because I couldn't yet count on myself, I would fall prey to my environment. Even if that environment wasn't frightening or hostile, I felt at its mercy, partly out of being a people-pleaser, partly out of growing up in an unpredictable school environment. You never knew when a punch or "fatso" would fly your way.

*   *   *

Bingeing and Purging

Back at home, with the kitchen inches away, I sent myself back into a bit of a feeding frenzy. I was also working some hours at catering, with some controlled eating and some complete eating tantrums. I had heard about bulimia… bingeing on mountains of food and then throwing it up. The idea sounded absolutely disgusting and painful, but it also seemed like a good remedy when an eating frenzy struck. I tried it for the first time that summer and got a rush from it. I dabbled with it, to greater and lesser extremes, over the course of the next seven years.

I can tell you that bulimia has nothing to do with losing weight and everything to do with feeling in control. Granted, I did it for the first time to keep myself from gaining weight after gorging for a good hour one night after my parents went to bed. I know that one night of overeating can't make you gain the weight you've lost, but I had become so hooked on the scale since moving back home (and the magic number it gave me every morning), I couldn't bear the thought of it going up instead of down. The scale has magic power to an overeater. It's like a fortuneteller and bad/good-o-meter rolled into one. *Being hooked on the scale and bingeing and purging gave me the same feeling…control.*

If I was experiencing a negative emotion, I could eat and eat and eat, then throw it up and feel better. I had instantly solved a problem. For the first few years I had no feelings of shame about the bulimia, only the joy of smothering my vague, undefinable emotions and then having no immediate consequence for it. It was like a drug in that it controlled my emotions. When I did start feeling shame about the bulimia, I could then feel bad about the throwing up rather than facing what was really bothering me.

The scale gave me the same feeling of control. When the number was lower, it was as if the little metal box was telling me I was good, that I had self-control. If the number was higher, I was bad, self-indulgent, and weak. Yet, I felt like I had control over the message I would get from the little metal box in the morning (one of the ways was through vomiting). Also, I didn't know how to give myself positive talk; I needed to get it from somewhere else. Even an inanimate object would do.

I would binge and purge about twice a week over the course of that summer, almost always late at night. When everyone was sleeping, I could creep outside, stick my finger down my throat, and puke into the tall grasses along the side of the country road near our house. Bulimia is reported to be a lot more common in women. This could be, but I would assert that it is more common in men than studies indicate. Men probably just don't talk about it.

I remember in high school hearing stories about the wrestling team eating and throwing up to maintain weight. I remember in ninth grade phy. ed. hearing one of the wrestlers throw up in the bathroom of the locker room every morning. Everyone knew he did it, but it wasn't considered an eating disorder. He was just tying to make weight for the wrestling match. This was a noble, manly pursuit. Eating disorders are probably as prevalent among men as they are among women; they just wear slightly different clothing. Can you tell me that sitting on a couch during a football game, drinking beer after beer, and eating your weight in chips isn't abnormal eating?

Elton John had bulimia, you know. He sought help for a triple addiction of cocaine, booze, and bingeing and puking. I heard in an interview that he would go on a multi-day coke bender then switch to eating and puking for a few days. I have no idea and am not in the position to guess the reasons behind Elton's bulimia, but I did see a recent interview where he spoke of the glories of coming clean. I do know that when there is turmoil in your life, bulimia adds a strange definition to all your problems. Somehow it reigns as king of issues, probably because it's so disgusting. Somehow, when I hear stories of the rich and famous suffering from it (Elton, Lady Di, Paula Abdul) it comforts me. It clearly is not a result of material scarcity in your life. ***It's a lack of love and caring for yourself.***

Bulimia is serious and is definitely an illness. I say this because the *idea* of vomiting when I've overeaten comes back to visit me to this day. Toward the end of my seven-year bulimia stint, I would start to feel crappier and crappier after puking. I guess my mortality was beginning to make itself known to me. I was scared of how I felt after a session; no longer was I elated and optimistic. I felt guilty, dirty, and pathetic. There are few things more disgusting than sticking your finger down your throat, tasting your own vomit, and then cleaning it up. I would also feel weak, exhausted, and dehydrated. My chest would feel tight, and my face would ache. Enough was enough. I was killing myself, so I vowed to stop. ***The really cruel joke about bulimia is it doesn't really work as a diet aid.*** Granted, you're getting rid of some of the thousands of calories you're inhaling, but not all of them. So the weight stays on. That fact alone I think is enough to make many a bulimic stop. The bulimia is keeping you fat.

Now, health experts would say that realizing you have an eating disorder and making a pact with yourself to overcome it is a great first step, but hardly a solid, complete plan. There is a lot of buzz about bulimia and the links to depression. Coincidentally, when I quit puking was when I started exercising regularly. Exercise increases serotonin levels in your brain, which combat depression, so without knowing it, I was fighting what I believe was depression with the exercise...and this natural antidepressant was helping me fight bulimia.

On the less healthy side, there was a period where I think I was literally replacing the puking with obsessive exercise (working out at noon and night), which I'll talk about later. But I think the trade was a fair and healthier one.

Also, if you want to stop bulimic behaviors, read about the side effects. It's kind of like watching the accident films in driver's ed. Tooth decay and gum disease are the least of your worries. Far worse are ruptured stomachs (from the bingeing, I assume), irregular heartbeats (from dehydration and potassium depletion), and swollen esophagus and salivary glands. Yuck!

*   *   *

A Massive Heart Attack in the Family

When I was a senior in college, my dad died of a massive heart attack. It came as a complete shock to all of us. There had been no warning signs that we know of, and Dad appeared to be in fine health. He was maybe ten to fifteen pounds overweight, nothing to be overly concerned about. He was also active and ate pretty well… fish, chicken, vegetables, and even red wine. He had high blood pressure, but it was being controlled with medication and had been for quite some time. It is important to note that his dad had died of nearly the same severity of heart attack at nearly the same age.

We were devastated. I remember one cold, late December night. It was dark, and the world seemed big, lonely, and frightening without one of my parents. (I think you get that feeling when a parent dies, no matter what your age. We think of our parents as always being around.)

There is a Midwestern custom of bringing loads and loads of food to a home where there has been a death. Neighbors had shown up at our door, barely able to speak. When words failed them, they simply held up a canned ham to substitute. We had more than 20 pans of Duncan Hines cakes, bars, brownies, and other desserts made of an array of Cool Whip, instant pudding, fruit cocktail, and graham crackers. People brought odd casseroles of tuna, noodles, and smashed

potato chips and salads made with conglomerations of beans, maca-
roni, and lots of Miracle Whip. Everything sat together on our utility
room table and oddly enough began tasting all the same. Someone
brought a big tray of sliced cheeses and meats. It was such a welcome
break from all the soupy, starchy affairs that my mom, my sister, and I
just sat around that cold night, grazing off the tray and talking about
my dad. We laughed and ate until the tray was gone. Maybe the amino
acids in the protein were helping to stabilize our brain chemistry.

The focus on the day of the funeral was on the making of the funeral
hotdish, Hamburger Hotdish, to be exact. Actually, I don't think it's
such a bad thing to focus on when you have such a difficult day to get
through. My mom led the mission, starting the day before by frying
the hamburger and chopping the onions and celery. These were then
mixed with tomato sauce, egg noodles, kidney beans, and corn and
put in enormous roasting pans that would be slipped into electric
roasters the next day by the ladies of the church. The scandal was that
the ladies of the church overcooked the hotdish, and it actually was
more of a soupy chili than a hotdish. Nonetheless, it was comfort food.

I brought Tupperware containers of it back with me when I
returned to college for my final semester and ate it for all my meals
until it was gone. It was, oddly enough, a strange final link to my dad.
As long as there was still hotdish left, my dad was still around. I ate it
even after it turned sour. I didn't want to let go of it.

David Letterman's heart bypass reminded me of my dad. As People
Magazine put it on their January 31, 2000 cover: "He's fit. He's thin.
He eats his veggies." So what happened to David? He was on a low-
fat, high-fiber diet and ran six miles the day before his diagnosis. He
did smoke, but a quintuple bypass at 52? Like my dad, David inher-
ited the heart disease tendency (his dad died of a massive heart attack
at 57). What is more important, I think, is the other thing David inher-
ited from his dad. People magazine also reported that like his dad,
David was "very, very worried about his work." (1/31/00, p.73)

Our dad was a big worrier. He worried about the injustices in the
world, about his past, about his kids, about his work…so many things.

His worrying most likely started when he took over the family farm at the age of fourteen. *I have no proof (except for the writing on the wall), but I believe that worry is the real killer.* What we think about most is what materializes in our lives. If your continuous thoughts are negative, sickness can't help but make a home in you. The really sad and ironic fact is I remember a talk that Dad had with me shortly before he died about the power of the mind to heal itself. I think he was just beginning to tap into this idea. I take it as one of the great lessons he taught me.

*   *   *

What We Tell Ourselves

There was an actor in the Theatre Department at Mankato State by the name of Ralph. He had to weigh at least 425 pounds. Ralph lived at home with his parents and claimed he stayed fat to get good character parts... but I say, "Bull."

Once, Ralph had a ragaholic attack in the dressing room. He became frighteningly violent...barking, scowling, and closing in on a freshman, who had apparently impersonated Ralph in front of others. Ralph's face grew beet red, and he was sweating, spitting, and shaking as he yelled. Poor Ralph disliked himself so much that the thought of someone imitating him made him go ballistic. Yeah sure, Ralph stayed heavy to get good parts. *We can come up with all kinds of reasons why we are fat.*

Katey Wirsch, a girl I knew in my undergrad days, was a Size 22 pear, who also claimed that she stayed that way because she was a character actress. Katey kept a list of men she had slept with that toppled over the 100 mark, like some growing list of intimacy. *Compulsive eating and sleeping with strangers have a lot to do with each other. Both numb your feelings, give you something else to feel guilty about, and give you a quick thrill and companionship at the same time. They both also keep real relationships and true intimacy at bay.*

        *   *   *

An Altered State

I was starting to make small, but rather significant changes in the way that I ate, but I was still a ways away from figuring out why I overate. One small step I took during my college years towards changing my mental processes in regards to eating was the use of self-hypnosis. The results were more hilarious than anything else.

One day I stumbled upon a rack of self-hypnosis tapes at the B Dalton bookstore in the Mankato mall. You could get one for just about every imaginable malady from smoking to nail biting to overeating. I thought I had found the answer, and I do believe there is validity to this approach; however, I also believe the same results are possible through positive self-talk and creative visualization (more on this later). My results were nightmarish, literally.

Every night while falling asleep, I listened to the tape for half an hour. All I heard was white noise, but subliminal messages were playing just loudly enough for my subconscious mind to pick up on. God only knows what was playing on this tape, but I woke up one night and swore I saw an enormous version of myself in a baggy, torn pair of white underwear, crawling out the bedroom window. This wasn't like a dream. It was more like a hallucination.

Another night while listening to the tapes I dreamt (but once again, it was very real) that I was driving along a lonely stretch of road in the middle of the night. In the headlights I spotted what looked like road kill lying on the road. As I came closer I recognized that it was me: pale-white, severely bloated, nearly dead with a gigantic slash across my belly. I stopped using the tapes.

As I said, this approach didn't work for me, but I've heard stories of it working for others, **and I think it did help me turn a corner in my** *weight loss journey by opening up to me the concept of looking inside my own head and heart to deal with my overeating.* It was a start, at least.

*   *   *

A Letter to Myself

Dear Eric,

It's time to start talking to yourself instead of someone else out there. What's wrong, Eric? Everything is going to be okay. Everything is going to be just fine.

 Whatever you are feeling, let yourself feel it. Listen to your emotions, and stop dismissing them as irrational and self-indulgent. Your feelings are your instinctive hard wiring and are to be listened to. They are desperately trying to tell you something. Insecurities do not make you different. Everyone has them; you are not strange or weird.

What are you putting on hold? What are you avoiding by constantly turning to food? Do you feel like you are going to disappoint someone? What kind of pressure are you putting on yourself? Are you still trying to prove that you are lov-able? What are the "shoulds" that you have in your mind that aren't doing you any good?

You are so lovable, Eric. When I step away and look at you, I just want to take you in my arms and hold you. Just by being alive, you are as worthy of love and happiness as anyone else on this earth.

Please, take care of yourself.

Me

*   *   *

Listening to Your Emotions

If there is only one thing that you realize from reading this book, I hope it is that your emotions are valid, real, and worth listening to. They are your gut instincts and your surest gauge of right and wrong. We get off track from trusting our own emotions and feelings when we begin to trust negative messages others tell us. We need to accept that they were acting off of their own wants and needs to get us to behave in a certain way. It is time to start listening to the heart of your emotions. Honor them. We have been taught all our lives to be honest. *Begin being honest with yourself. It makes life so much easier.*

I would assert that compulsive eating is mostly done to smother uncomfortable emotions. Compulsive or simple overeating really stems from our own hearts trying to tell us something through use of an emotion or feeling and our ignoring, squelching or dismissing that feeling as wrong. Instead of screaming our heads off, we stuff our mouths with food. *The only bad emotion is the ignored emotion.*

Why did I think I needed to hide my feelings over being picked on at school all those years? Who wouldn't have felt miserable over constant taunts and jeers? Instead, I told myself I was just being weak and oversensitive, that I should stick up my chin and turn the other cheek.

Why did I make myself feel at fault for not wanting to be on the football team or be a wrestler? Why did I feel like the misfit for not being comfortable hanging out at the end of the hall with the hot-rodders talking about cars? So what if I didn't want to learn welding in shop class (even though now I wish I had). *To this day, I still battle with more subtle forms of trying to please those around me.* At times I still act a certain way or try to be something that I feel is expected and would make me fit into the world rather than listening to my heart for guidance as to what I should do or be. The little fat kid trying to find his place in the world still surfaces.

Does your little fat kid still surface? We need to find ways to go back and get him or her, once and for all, and bring him or her with us. I think we do this by closely listening to our emotions and honoring them rather than honoring what we think is expected of us. Every time we say no to serving on a committee that just doesn't speak to us and say yes to taking a class that we have always wanted to, we honor our emotions. Every time we say no to more pay and more hours at work because it would rob us of precious family time, we honor our emotions. Every time we say no to a family reunion we don't want to go to and spend the time visiting family we want to see, we honor our emotions. The universe and God acknowledges honesty.

Consider treating yourself as you would a beloved child or your best friend. Think about the expectations you would place on these people, how you would advise these people in time of need and what level of patience you would exhibit when they screw up. You deserve treatment that is as kind, patient, and hopeful.

Part II

Figuring It Out...

Chapter 6

Wherever You Go, There You Are

After I finished college and then graduate school, I moved to Minneapolis. In my world, this was the big city. Just like when I went to college, I thought a change of scenery would make all the difference. Without the stresses and pressures of college (I had a lot to learn about what real stresses and pressures were), I figured I would finally be in the perfect mindset to lose weight, but that was not the case. ***I'm not sure the perfect mindset ever occurs.***

I was moving out on my own just as the fat free craze was sweeping the country. My friend Gina gave me a photocopied list of 500 or so foods with the amount of fat grams listed next to them. The buzz was you could eat anything you wanted and as much of it, as long as you kept your fat count down—around 30 grams a day. I could do this. Of course, the vegetables and green leafies didn't interest me as much as the breads and pastas did. I basically went on a four-year bread-and-cereal eating plan. I lost a couple of pounds through those years while feasting on breads, but it never clicked at the time that this style of eating wasn't really working for me to lose weight. I just assumed I wasn't losing much because I was eating a little too much bread and drinking a little too much beer and that things would kick in a week or so. I continued my walking, every other day or so for an hour, but I just camped out at around 265 (an interesting lesson on the necessary balance between exercise *and* eating right to lose weight). I was big but also flushed out from all the whole grain breads and pastas.

Actually, I became somewhat obsessed with the idea of flushing myself out. Perhaps it was an attempt to purge myself of bad feelings inside. I went on a mission to create the perfect bran muffin. I had it in my head that if I could create this fat free, colon-cleansing little treat that also tasted naughty, it would be my dieting trump card. At weak moments I could pop a bran muffin in my mouth. Oh, the rigor I put my insides through to achieve what I felt was perfection! It wasn't quite fat free, but it was close, and damned good. However, no matter how low in fat or healthy the muffin was, I couldn't have five at one sitting and still lose weight. To this day it is one of my favorites, but I eat one because I love how it tastes, and the gnarly texture is very satisfying. Well, maybe two, but definitely no more than three.

This was also the period when I became hooked on drinking a lot of water. Water is a good and necessary thing in one's life, and no harm can be done by drinking a lot of it, but I obsessed. Within the course of a couple weeks, two big girl dieters I knew sang the praises of drinking water. One had learned it from Weight Watchers and merely told me to drink "lots of it." The other said that you could lose weight just from drinking a lot of water. Technically, water does aid in weight loss (through flushing and raising your metabolism), but I took it as marching orders to flush and flush some more. I had just begun a stint as an administrative coordinator something or other at AT&T, a job that was to tie me over until I saved some money but lasted for five years. The job was monotonous, so I literally occupied my days by challenging myself to see how much water I could drink. I had one of those you-get-to-keep-the-cup gigantic tumblers, and I would drink at least 15 in a day, keeping a tick system going on a post-it note. Luckily there was a water cooler within fifteen feet of my desk and a bathroom within twenty.

Once again, I want to re-iterate that drinking a lot of water and fitting it into your life is a great thing, but I was using it as a fix. Much like the bran muffin fetish, ***I was trying to cleanse myself of what my*** *fat represented in my mind—shame, guilt, weakness, betrayal, and secrets.* Enough water and bran would get rid of it. When I drank a lot of water I envisioned the fat moving, breaking up, and leaving my body somehow. Not a bad creative visualization technique to latch on to. However, I don't believe that I was ready to let go of the bad feelings, so I ate and ate.

*   *   *

Treating Myself Like A Garbage Can

I would assert that, at any given moment, every fat person has one great behavior that is keeping him or her fat. Growing up, it was my mindless feeding from supper to bedtime. In college it was fast food frenzies. After college it seemed to be a couple of different things, both resulting from a job I hated but was too scared too leave. While at AT&T, I developed two habits that kept me fat—going to happy hour and eating out of the garbage. Seriously!

When you are bored with, find no joy or purpose in, and generally despise what you do eight hours a day, you get caught in a trap of laziness. You need an outlet, something to look forward to, and since you are in a sort of lazy cycle already, the happy hours that dot the bars around most corporate complexes are an instant, accessible, and reasonably cheap outlet. At AT&T we would have a happy hour a couple of times a week… usually at Chi-Chi's and sometimes at Stonewings, which was a bar in the nearby Tony Roma's rib joint. Both places had cheap drinks and free food.

The topics of conversation started with bitching about work and how unfair we were being treated and segued to dream talk about what we really wanted to do in life. At Chi-Chi's we would order $2.75 Fishbowl Margaritas on the rocks (bottom-barrel tequila-laced corn syrup) and eat baskets of free chips with ketchupy salsa, beans that looked like dog food, and cheese dip with a thick hard skin. I would begin each happy hour with the grandest intentions of a doing a little socializing and having a little fun before going home to get some stuff done. I would vow to have only two margaritas and a few chips. The cheap tequila quickly killed any aspirations of a positive evening, and by the end of the third margarita and probably the fifth basket of chips, the entire table sat in a glazed coma of guilt and depression.

Happy hours at Stonewings were just as sad but even stranger, if that's possible. Drinks consisted of cheap tiny beers and watery cocktails such as rum and cokes or vodka tonics. The food was set up in buffet style, heated with burning Sternos that filled the air with a gassy smell. We ate our weight in free cheese, olives, deep fried wings, and other appetizer oddities. Like happy hour at Chi-Chi's, everyone left very sad. Sometimes I would stop at the grocery store on the way home to get the makings for an ice cream social, a ritual that was a remnant of my bulimic days. If I binged on the ice cream, I would have something solid to feel guilty about.

Happy hours helped keep me fat those five years at AT&T. They were a vicious little Catch 22 that gave me something fun and exciting to look forward to throughout the day but left me drunk and depressed.

My second behavior that kept me fat stemmed from my noticing the incredible amounts of food being wasted by Corporate America. While I was at AT&T, it drove me crazy to see how much perfectly-good food was being thrown away every day. Now, it's better to throw the food in the plastic garbage can than to make yourself the garbage can and throw it in you, but something needs to be done about the excessive food mentality in the American workplace. Gigantic muffins and pillow-sized bagels are carried in for the morning meeting. Aluminum pans heaped with LeeAnn Chin Chinese food are delivered for lunch, and the remnants sit around all day in the lunchroom. Middle management has caught on that it is useful to numb employees with food—it makes the masses less resistant to change, and it's a relatively cheap way of making them feel special. These brunches and lunches at AT&T were free, but the old adage that there is no such thing as a free lunch could never have been more true. Like when we were kids and our lunches were set in front of us (pizza and green beans from the cafeteria), we become caught in the trap of thinking that whatever is given to us is good enough to eat. A mega-bagel for breakfast and chicken stir-fry for lunch in quantities limited only by pride creates stuffed, lethargic employees with hidden guilt over how much they ate. They shut up and slink back to their cubes for the rest of the day.

I ate out of the garbage at AT&T. This may have been my real rock bottom. Usually, it was pizza. The sales managers would order them at the drop of a hat for a "get fired up" meeting or when the team made their mark or for no real reason at all. They would order a ton, practically one large pizza per sales rep. Many would go uneaten and end up thrown away. I learned to keep an eye out for the salvageable food. I knew which garbage can would most likely have a hidden treat and when it would show up. The pieces of pizza may have been a little dried out around the edges, with the little balls of sausage hard and coated with congealed grease, but they would still be in pretty good shape. Good enough for me. The garbage usually consisted of just waste paper and a few cans so it wasn't quite as disgusting as you might think, but it did represent a few negative notions about food that I still had in my head.

I didn't think I was worth the time and expense of getting myself a real lunch...healthy, fresh, something I really wanted to eat that held no threat of botulism. I also felt like a sort of food detective secretly searching out hidden sources of food, another indication that I hadn't accepted my right as a living, breathing person to eat decent food and enjoy it. It also represented food as something evil in my mind. I needed to embrace food, to make it a friend, an ally, not a dark partner in secret crimes. I was relating to food in the only way I knew how, picturing a con artist who offered a quick thrill but then turned around to stab me in the back.

*   *   *

Strange Comfort

There was a fella by the name of Frank with whom I worked at AT&T. He was one of the oddest-looking men I had ever seen…about five feet, four inches tall and close to 400 pounds. He had yellowy-blonde hair with gray roots and a large, puffy face. He drove a tiny, Ford Festiva with a back seat stuffed full of crumpled-up fast food bags. I never once saw him eat a real meal, but he would make several trips down to the snack shop and return with king-sized Hot Tamales, Snickers, and half-liters of Coke. He didn't eat his Hot Tamales one at a time, but poured them in his mouth in the same way he drank his Coke. Frank didn't drink alcohol. He was recovering, so he did understand addiction to a certain extent. He would come to happy hours from time to time, but he would never eat or drink. *I've heard it said that we are the least tolerant of in others what we hate most in ourselves. Mirrors can be painful, and sometimes we don't want to look.* I was often short and dismissive with Frank. Granted, he was a needy character who would pull up a chair in your cube and talk endlessly about every little thing in his life, but, to be quite honest, Frank made me uncomfortable because he possessed traits I saw in myself and hated… the compulsive eating, the fat, and the insecurity. Frank often talked about how much he hated being fat and asked advice from me on how to lose (I had lost a few pounds while I knew him). I would tell him he had to do some kind of exercise, even mall walking. He would say he couldn't because of his bad knees and back. I would suggest eating regular meals instead of constant snacking. He would tell me about how he had no time to, that he was busy working. Frank was getting too much comfort from being fat, albeit smothering comfort. I think he was doing what I had done all of my life. He was using his weight as a device to try to control the way people treated him.

When you're fat, people tend to expect less of you in work and in personal relationships. Fat can be a kind of label, a sandwich board that reads, "I'm having trouble dealing with the world and adjusting to life. Give me a break, cut me some slack, and be nice to me." This becomes a kind of drug and an excuse when you mess up, forget something, oversleep or don't make the effort. You dream of being thin and fit, of eating normally, of not having the weight or the overeating be an issue, but you don't want to give up your great excuse and comforter. Frank had been a professional chef before coming to AT&T, but I received the impression that he hated food and what it had done to him. He had spent a large portion of his life working with food without ever finding any true joy in it.

$*$ $*$ $*$

The Secret of Exercise

A workout room had opened in the office tower of AT&T. It was no Lifetime Fitness, but it had exercise bikes, a stair climber, a weight machine, and a scale. I started going down to the exercise room on my lunch hours and riding the exercise bike for about 40 minutes. This gave me ten minutes to change before the workout and ten minutes to shower and change back to my work clothes. I would shovel in my lunch while I worked, which was not a great way to eat and left me tired, hungry, and pretty unsatisfied, but the biking and the reading I did on the bike felt great. I also started to see some muscles developing in my legs.

Ginny (a work-friend who battled with weight) and I were commiserating one day about our bellies and our butts. She mentioned that she had done Jazzercise during the 80's (its heyday I believe) and had lost a lot of weight without really trying. She knew of a class that met near work. Along with another friend, we decided to give it a try. Jazzersize worked wonders for me and was a testament to the secret of exercise. I've heard it said numerous times, "The best exercise is the one you will do." If it feels like the right kind of exercise, it is the right kind of exercise. It is most likely causing you no injury, you are able to do it within your heart-healthy zone, and you will be consistent.

Jazzercise, which is an aerobics class using real jazz dance steps and done to popular music and show tunes, bridged a gap for me. We all have a life that we know we could have lived if things had gone differently, a dream that in all reality will never be fulfilled (even though I do believe whole-heartedly in miracles). Mine is to have been a dancer. I really believe this. Even at my heaviest I could move with grace and confidence. In graduate school, at 300 pounds, my dance teacher praised my natural talent. If things had gone differently in life, if I had grown up where I would have had access to classes and dance opportunities and someone could have seen this potential in me and nurtured it…and if I hadn't been so fat… I would have been a dancer. Who's going to see dance potential in a little fat boy? I think that is why so many men are drawn to sports as their favorite exercise. It makes a connection to a fantasy self, a path that their life could have gone on, but didn't. Running does this for many. It's a chance to literally run away from your problems. And exercise actually does make problems go away, or at least seem less pressing.

Exercise should be fantasy time, a release to our higher selves when we are inspired to be all we can be and all we could have been. Jazzercise did this for me. It was also the most aerobically challenging exercise I had done since dance class in graduate school. I loved doing it so much that I became lost in myself, which was not only physically beneficial, but a great stress reliever. Because I was enjoying myself so much, I returned to class faithfully three times a week. I would have gone more if it had been held more often. *Exercise that connects to our spirit is exercise that we will make a part of our lives.*

Success breeds success. I was dropping pounds and gaining muscle from the Jazzercise, and, because I genuinely enjoyed doing it, my weight loss seemed to be happening without any strenuous effort. Once I saw and felt these changes, it made me enthusiastic and confident about the prospects of having the body I had always envisioned for myself. I began to re-examine how I ate. *People who have been overweight all their lives really don't believe that they have the power to lose weight.* They need to be convinced, to see proof, but, unfortunately, their doubt prevents them from giving it enough of a try to see results. *So much trust is required in the first weeks, even months, of a weight loss plan.*

*   *   *

How Much Was I Really Eating?

Up through my early twenties, I thought losing weight was done through abstinence. The less I ate, the better, and no food was the best. Then in my mid-twenties, thanks a lot to the fat-free food craze, my attentions turned to devising how much I could possibly consume and still lose weight. *I needed to take an honest and realistic look at just how much I was really putting in my mouth.* I had been dieting for the greater part of my life. Oddly enough, because of this, I was in denial over just how much I was eating. "I am a dieter. I can't be eating that much." Sadly, the joke was on me.

You read in so many diet advice books to keep journals of what you eat in order to get a handle on it. I always pooh-poohed such advice whenever I read it, thinking I was beyond such an elementary exercise. Well, I broke down and did it for a few days and was humbled and horrified. I read what I had written to one of my friends, who also wrestled with weight issues, and even as a fellow overeater she was shocked. After reading a day's entry to her, she asked in all sincerity, "Was that for the week?" I was lucky to have maintained the weight I did all those years, and I'm sure it was the sheer strenuousness of Jazzercise that was now making me lose.

A couple of thoughts entered my head that sound a bit harsh but clarified the entire situation for me. *It became clear to me that eating all that food was simply wrong, gluttonous, and selfish.* Under the principles of spirituality and the power of the universe that there are riches enough in this world to go around to everyone, I was quite literally eating another person's share. This wasn't the Depression. When I wanted more food, it would be there for me. I could trust this fact.

Also, the way I ate disgusted me. I imagined how I would feel if I saw this behavior in another person. I would feel sorry for him and wonder what was so terribly wrong in his life that he had to wallow in food and could not move beyond his addiction. Quite simply, I did not want to be him.

Moving beyond the denial and taking an honest look at what you eat everyday is actually comforting and inspiring if you let it. You will probably realize that there is no possible way that you could be any thinner while ingesting the amounts you are.

I always looked upon healthy eating and weight loss in such immediate, momentary terms. If I ate something bad, I would run to the scale and see if I got away with it. I would weigh myself every morning, and if I had eaten a lot the day before and hadn't gained weight, I'd gotten away with murder. If I had gained weight, I was bad and would decide to eat nothing all day to return to the weight that I was the day before. Oh, the time and energy spent balancing myself on the scale. Needless to say, I'm much better off without a scale in my life. Besides sending me into a false euphoria or self-defeating funk, it just isn't an accurate or dependable determinant of fat loss. You can tell just as easily by looking in the mirror if you honestly look and really see what is there. Plus, my weight fluctuates wildly from retaining water. Also, my little sneaking visits to the scale had me tricked into thinking that I could sneak handfuls of cookies, pieces of cheesecake, and candy bars and still lose weight. *After years of sneaking and checking the scale, along with intermittent longer periods of healthy eating, I realized that it's what a person eats over a longer period of time that determines weight loss (or gain).*

*   *   *

The Cabbage Soup Diet

Speaking of retaining water, I discovered a funny little week-long eating plan called the Cabbage Soup Diet. It had become a sort of urban legend that lived on photocopied pages and chat rooms on the Internet. I had heard it was originally developed for overweight hospital patients who needed to lose a lot of weight for surgery. Needless to say, it's not the greatest choice for losing weight because it is not a balanced eating plan that you can sustain the rest of your life. And it certainly does not celebrate the joy of food. Every time I've done it I've lost about five honest pounds, three pounds of real fat and I would guess a couple of pounds of extra water I was carrying around. The basis of it is a soup that you make and eat every time you're hungry. It's actually a pretty good soup. The recipe is:

> 1 head of cabbage, finely chopped
>
> 2 green peppers, finely diced
>
> 1 stalk of celery, finely diced
>
> 1 bunch of parsley, finely chopped
>
> 2 bunches green onions, finely chopped
>
> 2 packets of dry onion soup mix

Combine all ingredients in a stockpot with enough water to cover the ingredients, and bring to a boil. Reduce to medium and cook for three hours. Add salt, pepper or any seasonings that you wish. Garlic, curry, and hot peppers are all good choices.

You may have this soup whenever you wish, as much as you like, but other eating for the week is limited to the following on the given days:

> *Day One.* Unlimited fruits, but no bananas.
>
> *Day Two.* Unlimited veggies, but no corn or peas. A baked potato with a pat of butter for supper.
>
> *Day Three.* Unlimited fruits and veggies, but no bananas, corn or peas.
>
> *Day Four.* 5 bananas and a half-gallon of milk.
>
> *Day Five.* Up to 20 ounces of ground beef and unlimited tomatoes.

Day Six. Up to three steaks and unlimited veggies, but no corn or peas. You may substitute a chicken breast for one of the steaks.

Day Seven. Unlimited brown rice, veggies (but no corn or peas), and unsweetened fruit juice.

The absolute forbiddens during the week are bread, booze, and carbonated beverages.

I have morphed the mundane and rather uninspired Cabbage Soup Diet into a week long "spa" eating plan that gives me the sense of pampering myself while getting me back on a sensible, healthy eating regime. My spa soup is the same basic recipe as above but also uses my favorite, exotic spices such as cilantro, basil, minced ginger, and lots of fresh ground pepper. The week at the spa goes like this:

Day One. Eat unlimited amounts of your favorite exotic fruits, making sure to include watermelon, cantaloupe, kiwi, mango, fresh pineapple, fresh strawberries and raspberries. Make as many fruit smoothies as you wish with your favorite fruits. Blend your chopped fruits with a little water and chopped ice. Add a little Sweet and Low if you wish. Remember, no bananas.

Day Two. Have unlimited amounts of veggies, but no corn or peas. Celebrate the best of the fresh veggies (broccoli, cauliflower, artichokes, green beans, baby carrots, cucumbers, and red peppers). Eat them raw with a spritz of balsamic vinegar or steam and eat them with the tiniest dollop of Brummel and Brown yogurt spread, fresh ground pepper, and a squirt of lemon. You may eat a baked potato with chopped green onions and fresh ground pepper for supper.

Day Three. Combine days one and two, but no bananas, corn or peas.

Day Four. Use 5 bananas and a half-gallon of milk to make banana and milk smoothies: Blend a banana, 1/2 cup of milk, crushed ice, and a little Sweet and Low. Sprinkle a little nutmeg and cinnamon on top for color.

Day Five. Eat up to 20 ounces of ground beef and unlimited tomatoes. Grill your ground beef with some Worcestershire sauce.

Check out the seasoned diced tomatoes at the market and slice the best, fresh tomatoes you can find. Enjoy.

Day Six. Eat up to three steaks and unlimited veggies, but no corn or peas. You may substitute a chicken breast for one of the steaks. Splurge on a great steak, marinate your chicken breast in orange juice, and, what the hell, throw in a little seafood (shrimp and scallops…it has never affected my weight loss). Repeat your favorite veggies.

Day Seven. Use unlimited brown rice, veggies (but no corn or peas), and unsweetened fruit juice. Make a faux brown rice pudding with cinnamon, Sweet and Low, and a splash of milk. Yummy and soothing. Do a lo-cal fried rice by sautéing rice and veggies together and flavoring with curry (and throw in a few raisins). Finish up all of your favorite veggies from the week. Make fruit juice slushies in the blender with fruit juice and ice. Squeeze your own orange juice with strawberries and lemon added.

I include this diet not because I think it's something you should regularly incorporate into your life, but because I have found if I've had a week when I've overeaten a lot and feel puffy (like post-Christmas and New Years), it really helps me get a handle on healthy eating. I also know that whenever I finish a week of it, I ask myself why I don't eat more like this all the time. The fresh fruits and vegetables and lean meats taste so fresh and wonderful. **It can also give you an encouraging little jump-start to weight loss, which is only natural to need.**

*   *   *

In his book *How to Get What You Want and Want What You Have,* John Gray (the *Men Are from Mars and Women Are from Venus* guy) talks about the significant changes that occur in us at the age of 28. If we have emotional issues from our past that haven't been confronted for some reason, this is when they rear their ugly heads and demand resolution. *What is probably most significant is that we begin to turn inward to make necessary changes. Other people can help us, but ultimately we look to our own hearts for what we need most.*

For me, the age of 28 brought a year of powerful change. I think it was prompted mostly by the realization that I wasn't getting any younger, and if I wanted to accomplish goals and realize dreams I had envisioned for myself, I needed to get past this roadblock of overeating. The approaching 30's seemed to dictate an empowerment of myself, that I no longer needed to listen to others for the answers I was seeking, and that I needed to call upon myself for the things I wanted in life. *Simply put, I decided to take responsibility for my own happiness.* Why did it have to take 28 years?

*   *   *

Visualizing What You Need and Want

Out of the blue, a friend gave me a book: *Creative Visualization* by Shakti Gawain. I had heard the term "creative visualization" thrown around a little, but the concept seemed too good to be true. Could I actually attract into my life whatever I desired simply by visualizing it in my mind? Not in my consciousness.

By the second paragraph of the book, I could tell it was going to open up my life to me. It seemed to be directly addressing thoughts that I had swimming around in my head for the last 28 years—thoughts of not being good enough and having to settle for whatever I thought was handed to me or that good things only happen to others. I believe that these are thoughts common to overeaters and people who have grown up overweight.

The concept of creative visualization made so much sense and at the same time felt so right. It works off the principle that everything in the universe is made up of energy, and like energy attracts like energy. *When we create something in our mind, it then exists on the spiritual plane. By focusing our attention on it and surrounding the image with positive and loving thoughts, we actually attract it into the physical realm.* It's really just basic physics.

What makes it magical is that it works only for good in the universe, and it re-establishes our connection to the divine universe, or God, if you will. Finally all I had heard in Sunday school and endless confirmation classes was making sense. God was not a fickle, wish-granter in the sky, but a loving partner in my life who created with me all I needed or desired, as long as it was for the greater good. *The Bible was starting to make sense to me as well.* The power of creative visualization is referenced everywhere in the Bible. Matthew 7:7 states: "Ask, and it shall be given you; seek, and ye shall find; knock, and it shall be opened unto you."

Controlling what came into my life seemed to be less important, and accepting what could and did come into my life prevailed. I'm still an infant when it comes to attracting good into my life, but accepting myself as a student of life keeps me open to continuously searching for all the possibilities. I recommend buying this magical and inexpensive book (I saw it at the Barnes & Noble used-book section for $2). Creative visualization helped me see the two fundamental thought processes that were keeping me fat. Both stemmed back to my growing up years, and both needed to be addressed.

The first was quite simple but quite powerful at the same time. It was a basic impulse to eat when I was feeling like I was not in control, a Pavlovian knee-jerk impulse. This could be when I was feeling vulnerable, frightened, confused, uncomfortable or even joyous, ecstatic or excited. *Whenever an emotion that was heightened in the least entered my soul, I felt the impulse to put something in my mouth.* The reason for this impulse was no doubt complex and varied, and most definitely learned.

A bit of it may stem back to the colicky baby I was and the natural tendency towards sensitivity to external stimuli with which I believe I was born. Emotions are so heightened in some people, it's scary. Some of it no doubt also comes from growing up in a household where food was prevalent, always accessible, and often used as both a source of celebration and a pain-reliever. If you don't know what to do with a crying baby, tantrum-filled toddler or a child depressed from being teased at school, give him or her something to eat. This eating in the face of adversity becomes habitual and familiar. Pretty soon the behavior is an impulse. *My mom has said to me countless times that I sometimes look like I don't even know that I am eating. So how does one short-circuit this behavior? You begin by trusting that you can.* Learned behavior can be unlearned. I marvel at the human capacity for change.

Gary Zukav, author of *Seat of the Soul*, challenges us to feel the emotion when it comes to us. To not feel an emotion is to not tell the truth. *I think it's common in people who have grown up overweight to feel that there is something wrong with experiencing emotions.* Often, to guard yourself against teasing and the cruel comments of others, you need to turn off your emotions. To experience your honest feelings when being teased or rejected is nearly unbearable. Zukav says that when we experience an emotion, particularly an uncomfortable one, we should acknowledge it to ourselves in a very simple way, "I am confused" or "I am scared." By acknowledging and clarifying the emotion, we diffuse the power that it has over us. Then consider the wonderful and very real ideal of taking a positive turn on the emotion. If you are mad, try understanding and forgiveness. If you are anxious, breathe deeply and explore the calming effect of patience. The more and more you do this and resist the temptation to search out food, the less often the impulse to eat occurs.

The second basic thought process I needed to confront deals with tapes I had playing in my head that were remnants of growing up. Tapes that started out "I don't deserve...Bad things will happen...People won't like me" were most likely recorded in my junior high years. It began occurring to me that these tapes were actually quite selfish, self-indulgent, and rather lazy impulses with which I had become comfortable. They kept me from taking risks, trying new things, and getting close to people. I began replacing the tapes with new messages like "This organization is lucky to have me as an employee" or "I'm experienced enough at life to figure this out." Once I accepted a few basic ideas, I was further able to begin making positive changes in my life in regard to eating:

First, not everyone is going to like me, and when someone doesn't seem to respond favorably to me, it does not mean I am doing anything wrong. Other people's reactions to us usually say more about how they feel about themselves than how they feel about us. Remember Ruiz's *The Four Agreements*. We are the surest and truest judge of our own thoughts and actions.

Second, God and the universe are fair and want me to have my heart's desire. I sabotage my own path in life by holding on to pain from the past. What we dwell on the most is what we attract into our lives. I deserve and am worthy of good things.

Third, overcoming hurt from the past and moving forward in life is not a luxury. It's a right, and most importantly, a responsibility. We don't *have* to take responsibility for our lives. We *get* to.

I was using fat to put my life on hold, not because I was fat, but because I was choosing to hide in it and use it as an excuse for not taking chances in life. I was also holding onto it as a way of controlling others. "If someone doesn't like me, it must be because I am fat."

*   *   *

Dear Eric,

What if you stopped looking at the pain of childhood as a sentence to continue feeling that pain throughout your adult life? What if you no longer thought of yourself in the way that all the mean kids (and consequently you) thought of yourself: disgusting, out of control, a loser, and unlovable?

What if you finally accepted that living is a matter of bringing good things into your life, rather than suffering with what you think has been handed to you?

What if you gave up balancing on the scale for approval and looked to yourself and the positive changes you're making in your life?

What if you made all your eating and living choices based on the idea that you were going to live to be 100 and you loved the idea?

What if you woke up and expected great things to happen? What if each morning you said, "Something great is going to happen to me today. What's it going to be?"

What if you reminded yourself that you are responsible for your own happiness? The way you say something or don't say something, the way you walk or the expression on your face, cannot determine the happiness of others. They have to do that for themselves. What if you stopped making other people's decisions for them?

What if you remembered that feeling a little bummed or getting upset doesn't make you unlovable? It makes you an honest, real, and very lovable person.

What if you remembered you have a right and responsibility to take a break for a few minutes…or hours…or days?

What if you realized you don't have to eat everything you see? It will be there later.

Everything is going to be okay!

Love,

Me

Chapter 7

Eleven Truths I Discovered from My Years of Struggling with Food

1. *Men and boys are often ignored in the battle with food and weight.* When you're a little boy or an adult man, being a big eater has a certain status in our society. Statements such as, "He eats just like his father" and "He's going to be a football player" ring in the ears of the male eater, encouraging him to eat even more. As a result, if an eating disorder exists in a male, it is often ignored or unnoticed. Also, being a big boy or a big man sometimes creates the image of stature or power that a lot of men seem to enjoy and is praised in subtle ways. When a man realizes that he no longer wants to be fat and eat unhealthy, there isn't a lot of immediate support. No one is leaping forward saying, "Yes, I understand you need help." ***This is all made more confusing and conflicting by the health warnings that men receive.*** The dangers of obesity or being overweight are pointed directly at men. Heart disease, diabetes, colon cancer, and joint problems are all conditions or diseases commonly and frequently linked to either weight problems or poor eating habits. As a man you receive the mixed message, "It's important to not be overweight, but big eating makes you a man."

*　　　　　　　*　　　　　　　*

2. *Women have their specific issues as well.* Though the big shoulders and lean waist dream for men is certainly prevalent in our society, the ideals put out by the media for women to follow are even more prevalent. Print ads, television ads, and Hollywood are full of anorexic women. Those that aren't anorexic are artificially enhanced. No woman could live up to these standards in the real world. Also, although men are praised or considered macho for being big eaters, women who eat a lot are often thought of as gluttonous or out of control.

*   *   *

3. *No one wants to be fat.* I assert that if someone is overweight, he or she is very aware of it and want to lose weight. The preaching that you hear by some overweight individuals about the respect for and the rights of fatties is not coming out of a desire to be fat, but rather from a plea for acceptance (good for them). This no doubt comes as a necessary response to all the "there's something wrong with me" thinking out there.

*   *   *

4. *Overeating and compulsive eating are basically the result of denying emotions.* Somewhere along the way, we got it into our heads that our emotions are silly and not worthy of a listen. Because they are very real, necessary, and significant, our emotions must get out somehow. Overeaters turn to food in forms of eating tantrums when the act of denying their emotions becomes too overwhelming. Eating also numbs the confusion and unrest that comes from second guessing these emotions.

*   *   *

5. *Success breeds success in weight loss.* You simply have to see some success to inspire you to continue. If you've been overweight all your life, you need to see some results to believe you can ever be your ideal weight. It's all well and good to make eating healthy and living well your goal, this is a worthy goal, but it's human nature to need some inspiration along the way and to need it quick. This means that the first week or two of healthy eating will be tough, and the first few days will be very tough. You simply have to accept the fact that it will take a while for results to appear. Not seeing immediate results has caused me to overeat thousands of times. Believe me; the scale will move and the pants will loosen, but you need to allow yourself a generous kick-off period.

*   *   *

6. *You have to find the joy in food.* Food is not a bad thing. It is a wonderful, joyous, exciting, creative, and, not to mention, necessary thing. Doesn't it make sense to embrace it and celebrate it since it isn't going and can't go away? We can live without cigarettes, booze, and drugs, but food is here to stay. Make a list of your favorite foods and search for ways to make them lower in calories and fat, or eat them sparingly or in small portions, but eat them. Whenever I have a cheeseburger with onions (a personal favorite) for lunch, it flips the satisfied switch in my brain, and I don't want Hot Tamales and buttered popcorn in the afternoon. This is partly from getting ample protein and partly from getting what satisfies me.

*   *   *

7. *A lot of the good that exercise does will not show until you've dropped some pounds.* I went through a period when I was faithfully committed to stomach crunches, but nothing was showing, and my saggy gut just hung there. Then I lost about ten pounds, and, surprise, the stomach muscles slowly started to appear. If you're lifting or crunching, until you drop some poundage, the muscles are not going to show.

*   *   *

8. *A little obsession goes a long way.* Think of it as giving focus to a worthy cause. That worthy cause is your life. I've talked with so many overweight people who use the excuse, "I don't want to become obsessed with losing weight." My experience is that it helps to have somewhat of an obsessed attitude when you are starting out. I'm not talking about a crazed, psycho, can't-think-about-anything-but approach. However, it does take roughly two weeks to incorporate any new habit, so you do need to revisit your goals often during that time. This will allow you to see some success, which is very encouraging.

*   *   *

9. *Whatever weight you are, it is where you need to be to learn the lessons you need to learn*. I spent half of the fat years of my life denying my weight and the other half in misery over the reality of it. It wasn't until I saw the lessons that life was presenting to me that I lost the weight.

*   *   *

10. *You are okay exactly the way you are.* Get out of the golden moment mindset, that undefined moment somewhere in the future when everything will be perfect, you will be thin and fit, and you will eat well and have no stress. Meditate on the sentence "Everything is okay exactly the way it is." It's amazing how things start to change when you do so.

*   *   *

11. *You're responsibility on this earth is to find true joy and experience real happiness*. Joy and happiness aren't nice little extras that sometimes coincidentally happen, usually to someone else. Joy and happiness are our birthright, and, consequently, our responsibility to embrace. Rediscovering our passions and that which truly excites us is the way to do this. Remember, you don't *have* to take responsibility for your life. You *get* to.

Chapter 8

Do You Really Want to Be Thin?

Of course you do. Who doesn't want to be thin? But the real question to ask yourself is **"Am I willing to give up what I'm getting in return from overeating and being fat?"** It took me a long time to see all the paybacks that I was receiving from keeping myself fat. On the surface I thought of being fat as a curse, a cruel edict from above, and being thin as the answer to everything. I needed to realize that we all have very real reasons for maintaining certain behaviors, even the bad ones. It ain't just a big coincidence.

When I ask myself what I need to give up, it usually comes down to needing to be liked by everyone. I think this is common in overeaters. Years of teasing and feeling bad about yourself have shifted your sense of self-worth over to others. In the face of continuous rejection, it becomes a mission to try to present yourself in a way that will receive a positive response in others, no matter what your true feelings are. But the denial of our true selves does so much damage. We lose a connection to what we truly feel and truly want in life. We no longer trust our truest inner voice, our own heart. We lose confidence in our ability to meet and deal with the challenges life presents us. And because our sense of self-worth is based on other's opinions and responses, our happiness is at the mercy of others. Food numbs the pain that this cycle creates and is our friend when others appear to betray us. **The**

even scarier question to ask ourselves is, "What if I lose the weight and people still don't like me?" If we have other aspects of ourselves that may need a little adjustment, keeping ourselves fat also keeps us from facing these. The constant pursuit of being liked by everyone also helps us avoid the parts of ourselves that we need to face.

Why would we want everyone to like us? If we are being true to ourselves, there is no possible way that everyone is going to like us. As a matter of fact, if everyone does like you, it's a sure sign that you're not living the life of the creative, expressive, smart, opinionated, free-spirited, capable, independent individual you were meant to be. It's time to make needing to be liked by *you* the priority. It's a scary thing if you've never done it, but a sense of peace and relief washes over you when you think about not needing to have everyone like you. Say it to yourself, "It is not my job to have everyone like me." **Once you realize that it's more important to like yourself, you begin living like someone people will like.** It can be the most powerful personality makeover there is.

*   *   *

Be willing to give up controlling the way that people react to you (and controlling people in general). Perhaps you have learned, as I had, that the way you look draws a certain reaction from people. I used fat as a way to be less accountable for my actions. If I stayed fat, I figured that people would continue to see me as troubled, vulnerable, sad, and sensitive and as a result would expect less of me in personal relationships, family affairs, and work. "We can't expect too much of Eric. He's a big, sensitive guy. Be nice to him." It was my way of keeping people at bay. My layer of fat was acting as an insulator between me and the world. However, I wasn't just insulating myself from the pain. I was insulating myself from the real joy that comes from getting in touch with who I really am.

My fat appearance went hand in hand with a sort of feigned happiness. I kept up an on-the-surface, drunk-like stupor of silly happiness, hiding my real sadness, which kept people from taking me too seriously and kept myself from risking too much in relationships and in my professional life. A constant smirk can act as an honesty repellent. It seemed comfortable and safe at the time, but it was ultimately robbing me of true joy and any solid level of success. I never learned to truly trust who I was on the inside, and when I did get some negative feedback from someone or encountered some genuine conflict, it terrified me. Every remark was a personal attack.

Perhaps you use your size to the reverse of what I did, as an intimidation factor. Some overweight folks threaten others with their size by presenting themselves as stoic (or else boisterous) giants. This device also robs you of any authentic joy because it is not a true representation of who you really are.

As mentioned earlier, growing up fat makes you feel like an outsider, and constant teasing makes you feel unacceptable and unloved. The acceptance of others becomes a goal, and you teach yourself that behaving the right way will receive a positive response from others. Consequently, if someone reacts to you in an unfavorable manner, it's rejection, and it smarts. Food comforts this.

When you stop using food as a drug and give up your size as a weapon against others, you make yourself vulnerable. Yet, in turn you begin to trust your own heart and your own mind. You discover your authentic self. It's a process indeed, but a process worth going through.

*   *   *

Be willing to give up being perfect and not making mistakes. In order to successfully give up controlling others with your fat, you will have to learn to be comfortable with not being perfect and with making mistakes. It seems like such a simple idea and one we've been reminded of constantly since we were tikes—"Nobody is perfect. Everybody makes mistakes." However, most adult fat kids have never fully grasped their right to make mistakes and not be perfect. Along the way we picked up the idea that if we do everything right and don't make waves, maybe then people will be nice to us.

Begin by meditating on the notion that there are no mistakes in life, only lessons to be learned and alternate paths to be taken. Where did the big, bad concept of the mistake come from anyway? In some stifling little grade school classroom, I'll bet. If you're not making mistakes (in the traditional use of the word), you aren't living life to your full potential. And in trying to be perfect, you are living your life with someone else as your ideal, which is an impossible and disastrous notion. Progressive businesses are learning that the philosophy of freeing people from the fear of mistakes is a valuable one. **Only in a safe environment can free thinking and creativity occur.** Not making mistakes is actually frowned upon because it's a sure sign that folks are not challenging themselves or taking risks. Without these two things, new growth cannot occur.

This lesson of giving up perfectionism presents itself time and again as one loses weight. **It is not the eater who strives to be perfect that loses weight and keeps it off. It is the eater who strays off the path from time to time but then promptly jumps back on. Eating healthy 80% of the time is a great goal.** Trust me here.

*   *   *

Be willing to give up relying on others and external forces to tell you how you should feel about yourself. Somewhere along the road we became out of touch with our own sense of self. Maybe it was from being fat all our lives and feeling so different and alone. Maybe it was from desperate attempts to be liked and accepted after being teased so much. Maybe it was from a sense of our bodies betraying us. Whichever it was, many fat people (myself included) transferred all sense of self-worth into the hands of others. This gives an incredible amount of our own power away and makes us feel helpless, a victim of life's circumstances. We get hooked on approval from others. We discover that a lot of people like to have other people dependent on their approval, so we receive favorable responses from them, and we keep going. **Addiction to the scale is a plea for approval from an inanimate object.** If the scale says I am a good boy, then I can feel good about myself.

Begin listening to yourself for approval. We all are born with a rock-solid gut instinct and a good sense of what is right or wrong for ourselves. Meditate on the notion of listening to yourself more than to others. Of course, we must be open to honest, appropriate, constructive, and respectful feedback and input from others. It's one of the surest ways to grow and learn. However, beware of giving away your power. Respect your own choices and heal yourself. Listen to your heart and respect what it says.

*   *   *

Be willing to disappoint others. There are, no doubt, people in your life who are happy with you being overweight, most likely because you are not challenging them to face issues and addictions of their own. Also, there are most likely people around you who have gotten hooked on your dependence on them (co-dependence). Remember, you're not doing them any favors by not being honest with them. The people in your life worth having around will stay with you as you lose weight. The rest are yesterday's news. More on this later!

*   *   *

Be willing to give up denying you have emotions, especially negative ones. You've probably learned to swallow your emotions like a hunk of cheesecake. Your emotions, good or bad, are trying to tell you something useful or helpful. Don't smother this valuable information with food. Dare to feel the emotion, get to the heart of it, and use it to propel you forward. The more you do this, the better you become at it. **A lot of us grown-up fat kids are conditioned to reach for food when conflict stirs up a bad feeling in us**...when we can't figure out our computer at work, when our car makes a weird noise, or when we disappoint someone. Somewhere back when we started reaching for something to eat, it felt good because we didn't have to think about the dilemma while we were eating. The rest is history. **When you've somehow gotten it into your head that you don't have the right to honestly feel whatever it is you are feeling, you can turn to food, eat a ton of it, and then feel bad about that. You instantly have something simple and solid to feel bad about instead of having to figure out more complex or murkier issues.** Instead, face the feelings and conflicts in your life, and the need to stuff yourself with food will begin to subside.

*   *   *

Be willing to give up being bored. There is a quote from Richard Bach that goes, "In order to be truly happy, one must sacrifice boredom. This is not always an easy sacrifice." I think of excess fat as unrealized potential, not just potential to be thin, but potential to be your true self and everything that the universe meant you to be. It's difficult to accept that the universe wants us to have everything we've ever desired. It does mean that we will have to give up doing what is comfortable and familiar for what is right.

So ask yourself again, "Am I willing to give up what I'm getting from overeating and being fat?" Yes, you are. It's time to cash in the old and tired ways of living to which you've grown accustomed for all the possibilities that living your true life can bring you.

Chapter 9

Do You Really Need to Lose Weight?

You know if you should, and you certainly know if you want to. Do your knees ache, grind, and sound like Rice Crispies (and you're only 30)? Do you get chest pains when you exercise or are forced to run? When you enter a room full of people, do you search for someone bigger than you? Does your stomach resemble a woman who is nine months pregnant? If you're a man, are you tired of having boobs? Do you constantly tug at your shirt to keep it from clinging? If you're a woman, are you tired of having huge breasts? Can you feel your heart beat faster from going up a single flight of stairs? Do you have over a 38-inch waist? Are you achy and stiff in the morning? Are you tired of your thighs chafing? If you're a man, does the thought of taking off your shirt in public mortify you? Do you avoid activities that are fun or interest you because of your size, for example anything that requires wearing a swimsuit or changing clothes in front of others? Has a friend or family member expressed concern about your weight? *Do you just want to be free from it all and be thinner?*

Does any of this sound familiar? Any one is a pretty good indicator that you may need to lose weight. For an objective point of view on whether you should lose weight, looking to the ideal weight charts (available from your doctor and in books and on websites all over the place) is an okay way to begin to determine a healthy weight. It will give you a general idea of what you should weigh. I'm also fond of the "dressed test." Most of us have little flabby areas that are visible when we're naked; it just doesn't matter unless we are swimsuit models. (However, let me note that if you want to do something about your little flabby areas, that's okay too.) But if you appear overweight while dressed, you are most likely sufficiently enough over your ideal, healthy weight to justify some attention. At this point, I wouldn't worry about what your ideal weight is, other than as a reference point. When you start taking care of yourself and making healthy choices for your body, you will return to the weight that is right for you.

We have all heard of the potential health risks of being overweight: heart disease, stroke, increased likelihood of certain cancers and diabetes, joint problems…to name a few. As damaging as these all are, ***I firmly believe that the most harm comes from being overweight and <u>wanting</u> to be thinner but believing that you are not worthy or could never be able to lose weight.*** The guilt that goes along with being overweight, the lowered sense of self-worth, the sadness, and the loneliness add insult to injury. These are the real damaging factors. Our minds have the power to heal us and to make us sick, and I believe that fat people mostly make themselves sick by desperately wanting to be thinner and not doing anything about it.

It is not self-indulgent to be concerned about your health, your appearance, and your general well being. It's actually self-indulgent to ignore these things. If you have a desire to lose weight, become fit, and eat healthier, you have every right and responsibility to yourself to do so. Your physical self may be pleading for you to lose weight, but your inner self is as well.

*   *   *

Ask yourself, is your eating or your size getting in the way of who you really are…your true self? If so, then please answer your soul's calling. Do you have joy in your life? Do you have areas of interest that remain unexplored? Perhaps you've abandoned interests, loves and passions along the way because of your size or because you somehow got it into your head that you don't deserve the joy that comes from them. Maybe some of these interests were abandoned as a child, and food became the replacement. *Fat people are very good at punishing themselves because they think they are lazy, weak slobs.* You're not, you know. You've just wandered off the track of who you are and into a rut you are able to get out of, starting here and now.

Honor your body and your soul. However, as far as the body goes, ignore the images of skinny models that are plastered around us in our world. Lighting effects and airbrushing are used abundantly to create images that seem idyllic but are difficult to achieve and impossible to maintain. We need to develop a lifestyle plan of eating and exercise that will stay with us throughout our hopefully long lives and will be such a true part of us that we won't have to think about it. Listening and obeying your own body's signals is the one true test. *Finding an exercise that you want to do nearly every day and finding foods that nourish your body and your soul (more on these two things later) will get your body to the shape and weight it was meant to be and will free up your mind and soul to live and experience a joyous life.*

To get started, you may need a goal weight. Once again, use the charts as a rough guide, but *start focusing on your lifestyle and trusting that your body will get itself to where it was meant to be,* and you will be everything you've dreamed of being: fit, healthy, attractive, sexy, and confident.

*   *   *

Begin by Creating Your Ultimate Self in Your Mind

Let's chat about this important concept. Creative visualization is a powerful tool in all aspects of your life and invaluable on your journey to weight loss. Shakti Gawain and Wayne Dyer have written wonderful resources on the subject. For fat people, the idea of creating something in your mind and then having the ability to bring it into reality can seem impossible to grasp. Years of teasing, verbal belittling, and feelings of your body betraying you can create a notion of scarcity in your life. Happiness seems to be a crapshoot or luck of the draw. Creative visualization invites you to put those feelings behind you and accept and acknowledge your right and ability to have whatever you need or want in life. Shakti Gawain presents these basics in her book *Creative Visualization*.

We must accept the physical principle that everything within the universe is comprised of energy, and by that very fact we have the ability to draw to us whatever we need or desire. Like energy attracts like energy.

We are not separate from everyone and everything. We are all comprised of the same energy within the same universe, and we are all connected.

All we want and desire already exists when we create it in our imagination. It is only a matter of attracting it to us and bringing it into the physical realm. Also, creative visualization only works with *love as the motivating force.*

Put all your censors and current circumstances aside and allow yourself to dream. Imagine yourself eating, exercising, living, and looking like you would ideally like. The first step to achieving your authentic self is to visualize it.

Imagine yourself with only your favorite, healthy foods in your pantry. What would you have for breakfast? Of what would your lunch consist? If you could create any dinner for yourself, what would it be? Would you have a fabulous glass of wine with it? Do you see yourself eating small amounts of your favorite treats, maybe something you abandoned years ago in the name of dieting? Do you drink plenty of good, fresh, cool, filtered water? Sounds heavenly; doesn't it?

How would you eat? Sitting down at the dining room table or on your porch or in your backyard, slowly, enjoying each mouthful, perhaps reading a little between bites? Is your favorite music playing? Do you make time for your meals, treating them like special occasions? Do you bring your lunch to work because you can't find what you want at the corner Super America? Do you bring your own coffee to work because you don't like the taste of the work coffee? Do you only eat what you enjoy? Do you stop eating something if it doesn't thrill you?

How does your body look? Do you take care of yourself, getting a haircut when you want and wearing clothes you love that feel good? Do you use hand and body lotion that you love? Are you healthy and fit with good muscle tone? Is your skin moisturized from drinking enough water? Do you move freely and strongly, able to run or jump when you need or want? Can you see your feet for the first time? Are your legs toned from running? Are your arms strong and lean? Is your stomach flat? Is your heart beating at a healthy rate?

Do you make time for your exercise? Do you look forward to your walk or run every day? Do you feel energized after yoga or stretching? Do you feel stronger and more relaxed than you ever have?

This visualization is a vital first step in becoming everything you dream. Dreams don't lie, and if we refuse to censor ourselves and instead dream with love in mind, our dreams will not lead us astray. **If what you visually create and dream about differs from your reality, then you should take whatever steps are necessary to achieve these dreams.** It is your right and responsibility to yourself to do so. Under the laws of a loving universe, if you make the first step, the universe will come to help you in more ways than you ever imagined possible. Exciting; isn't it?

*   *   *

Above all, remember that you are okay exactly as you are. That may seem contradictory. Just because you've got aspirations, dreams, and visions of who you ultimately want to be, aspects of your true self you still need to realize, it does not mean that there is anything wrong with you. **On the contrary, you will not move forward until you fully realize that you are okay exactly the way you are. Say it until you feel the calm and acceptance.** You are okay exactly as you are. Give yourself the unconditional love that everyone deserves. What a relief it is to finally realize that you don't *have* to lose weight and start exercising. You *want* to lose weight and start exercising.

*　　　　　　　*　　　　　　　*

Acknowledge the past

Part of accepting that you are okay exactly as you are is acknowledging the past. Instead of feeling bitterness over your past and all the things you may have lost or missed out on because of being fat, overeating, and other weight issues, reflect on the following statement: **You are exactly the size and weight you need to be to learn the lessons in life that you need to learn.** Concentrate on this thought. Life presents us with lessons and keeps presenting them to us until we get it. Instead of hating ourselves for years of overeating, doesn't it help to accept the possibility that we are where we are so that we can learn valuable things about ourselves that will make our lives fuller, richer, and more satisfying than we ever imagined possible? **Everything is as it should be at this moment in time, but it's also time to move on.**

*　　　　　　　*　　　　　　　*

A Creative Visualization Exercise for Weight Loss

One. Begin by making yourself comfortable, sitting or lying on the floor with arms and legs uncrossed. Breathing from your diaphragm so that your stomach and not your chest expands (also known as belly breathing), take five deep cleansing breaths, breathing in through your nose and out through your mouth. With each exhale, visualize tension leaving and your body becoming progressively more relaxed. When you have taken your five deep breaths, do one more conscious relaxation "wash" beginning at the top of your head and going through your entire body, imagining the tension dripping out of your toes.

Two. Begin to imagine yourself as you would ideally wish to be. See yourself in your favorite clothes or naked, moving about freely with spirit and energy. Imagine yourself calm and at peace. See yourself eating well and enjoying exercise. Focus on how it makes your heart feel. Feel the warmth, peace, joy, freedom, and love of becoming your true self. Enjoy this time. Let yourself go and visualize the ultimate you.

Three. Let your vision grow into a simple, positive affirmation statement that exists in the present. Examples include: "I eat only what I wish, and I am thin, strong, and confident." "I am worthy of being my ultimate self, which is lean, strong, and at peace." "I move with confidence and grace." "I eat only healthy foods that I love."

Do this simple exercise as often as you can…at least once a day and preferably twice, in the morning and the evening. ***The key is to keep the visualization active and present. Think of it often.*** Be as clear and concise with your visualizing images as you possibly can. The universe needs and wants to hear and see exactly what you need.

If negative or self-defeating images come into play, acknowledge them, and then gently tell yourself that you are choosing your new, positive way of being.

Keep your visualizations to yourself. They are between you and the universe. This is so important. The people I know who talk the most about spirituality and positive changes in their lives are the ones who just can't seem to get it working for them.

Keep a close look out for small changes appearing almost instantly, and trust that they will appear. Trust in the divine power of the universe is crucial.

Study *Creative Visualization* by Shakti Gawain or anything by Wayne Dyer for further information. I wish for you to become all that you are meant to be.

Chapter 10

Where Do You Start?

"Whatever you can do or dream you can, begin it.
Boldness has genius, power and magic in it. Begin it now."

—Goethe

*　　　　　*　　　　　*

Growing up fat makes you different. You look different, and you feel different. You also carry a lot of guilt about your eating and about being so big. You can't help but feel that you are a bad kid and that you are doing something wrong. I was certainly aware I was fat, but it just didn't make sense to me that people would be mean to me for that fact alone. In turn, I felt I was a bad, lazy, and dumb little boy. Unless we get some sort of closure on these kinds of feelings, they continue to haunt us and sabotage our attempts to lose weight when we're adults.

Once again, you are okay exactly the way that you are, and you are at the weight you need to be to learn the lessons that you need to learn. **Look for the sense of peace that comes from accepting yourself as is.**

Now, self-acceptance does not mean you have to settle for your body being the way that it is, but it does mean that you have to accept responsibility for allowing yourself to get in to the physical state that you currently are. **Self-acceptance also means that you believe in your ability to get in to the state that you visualize for yourself...your true self.** Remember, your overweight self is not your true self. It's a self you created out of dealing with the events of your life. No remorse or shame is necessary. You simply responded in the best way you knew how at the time, but you are now ready to accept that overeating is no longer the way you choose to respond to life. The fact that you're reading this book is proof of that.

*   *   *

What does food represent to you?

Why do you overeat? Food, in its purest form, is meant to sustain us. It is also wonderful for celebration and entertainment. However, food has grown to mean a lot more than these few things to a lot us. Some of the roles it has come to play include:

Friend. If you have a natural tendency towards shyness, food may have been your safest friend when you were a child. If you had trouble getting along with other children, food may have become your easiest friend. If you never felt like you fit in with other kids, food may have become your most comfortable friend. Over the years, as you grew up and began to make your way in the world, food became even more accessible to you, and responsibilities and pressures became greater, as they do in life. If you have not learned to accept your shyness or your feelings of being different and move forward, you will continue to overeat to ease the discomfort. Food continues to be a silent best friend. It asks nothing of you but gives you great, albeit temporary, comfort and companionship.

Entertainment. If your body size or your feelings of disconnect from your peers kept you from participating in group activities or lessened your self-confidence to the point where you abandoned interests in your life, food may have become an activity. I know that I considered eating in front of the TV to be my primary after-school activity while growing up. I was a creative, talented little kid who could have been doing so much more. I'm sure you were too. To this day, eating may be the only thing that you feel you really have to look forward to doing in life. Plus, no one can deny you have to eat, and food is always around.

Stress-reliever. Maybe you lived in a household where conflict was a norm, and at meal times everybody was too busy eating to argue. Mealtime was a quiet time, a happy and peaceful time. Were you the oldest child? You may have carried the burden of responsibility for the other children. Mealtime was the only time when you felt comfortable tending to your own needs.

If you grew up in an alcoholic family or with a moody parent, you may have never felt comfortable expressing your true feelings. You may have learned to survive by walking on eggshells, wearing your happy mask, and making as few waves as possible in an attempt to please your unpredictable parent. Food numbed the pain that came from swallowing your emotions.

Lover. If you were a fat teen, your dating years were quite likely far from ideal. Your healthy development as a sexual being couldn't help but be affected by your weight. Not only were you self-conscious of your body, but also society sends a powerfully shaming message about being overweight, so maybe you never felt accepted or acceptable. This all culminated in missing out on an important time in life. If you missed out on it, you know what I mean. If your sexual preference was for the same sex and you had no support system available, the confused, uncomfortable feelings were tenfold.

Instead of getting romantic attention from boys or girls, you were probably teased and made to feel ugly or even freakish. Not only did you learn not to trust these people with whom you were supposed to be developing relationships, but in your head your body was betraying you as well. To whom do you turn? You turn to your best friend...food. ***This is why overeating and casual, promiscuous sex have so much in common. Both are a quick thrill and source of comfort without any intimacy involved, and both leave you feeling emptier than before the eating or the sex.***

Protector. Ultimately, food became your shield, and not only did you turn to it in times of despair, but you also used it to create a protective barrier of fat. You found continuously greater comfort in eating, and soon your fat was a buffer to the pains of life. You used it as a painkiller, and it also became your great excuse. ***"As long as I'm fat, I'm not responsible for dealing with the other problems of my life."***

You don't make yourself vulnerable to love because you tell yourself that no one will ever love you anyway, at least in your current state. ***"When I get thin, I'll find love."*** Throughout all of this, you tell yourself there will be that golden moment, sometime in the great unknown ahead, when you will be thin and everything will be different. ***Life is not a dress rehearsal. There is no time to postpone joy. We deserve to be happy and have a responsibility to start being so right now, no matter where we are in life.***

*   *   *

Forgiving

The first step to finding closure to the issues that drove you to seek comfort in food is forgiveness. It's time to forgive those who wronged you (for whatever you feel resentment, not just issues related to food and fat). It's time to forgive your parents. Nobody comes out of life unscathed, and nobody ever promised us a perfect childhood. Your parents, with their shortcomings, were doing the very best that they knew how at the time.

Are you holding onto anger or resentment from your past? The boys or girls who were merciless to you in high school? The teacher who was unfair to you? The sibling who ignored you? The friend or lover who deserted you? Come up with your top five.

It's time for forgiveness. Forgiveness does not mean that you suddenly see your transgressor's behavior as acceptable. It does mean that you are letting go of the hold that the wrong has over you. Until you forgive the wrongs done against you, they remain cankers that continue to infect you and hold you back from everything that you could ultimately be. Focus on the fact that your wrongdoers have more in common with you than you think. They were merely fellow humans attempting to find their way through life as best they could, making mistakes and learning lessons along the way.

Holding onto anger for something someone did or said is, in essence, continuing to confirm that they were right. When you do not forgive, you remain mired in the world that was created for you by the cruel remarks or actions of others. You sentence yourself to the reality that was created for you. Don't you want to move on and create the reality that you imagine for yourself? Your ideal reality? Don't you think you should have the final say over how your life goes, rather than the thoughtless, fleeting remarks and actions of someone else?

*   *   *

You Get What You Decide You Deserve

Once you have begun the process of healing wounds from the past, it's time to start accepting the fact that you deserve to have whatever your heart desires. This includes ending your constant overeating, losing your excess weight, and becoming the individual you imagine yourself becoming.

As stated earlier, growing up fat makes you feel different from everyone else. Feeling different, especially as a youngster when it isn't necessarily a good thing to be different, makes you think you're alone in the world. (I think you first need to feel that you fit in before you can feel secure enough to be comfortable being different.) When you feel alone as a kid, you get the idea that you somehow have to earn the good things that come into your life, and even if you're a good kid, there's no guarantee that good things will come your way. This goes even for love.

Wayne Dyer writes in his book *Manifest Your Destiny* (a book I highly recommend, particularly to those of you who feel you "don't deserve") the steps to attracting into your life all that you desire. In addition to other vital principles (some of which were discussed earlier in the section on creative visualization) are three of particular note to those who have grown up overweight:

We are inseparably connected to our environment and the universe. (p. 38)

You are worthy of the abundance of the universe and all that is in it. (p. 73)

Unconditional love connects you to manifesting your destiny. (p. 93)

Your need for food to fill a role in your life, other than to sustain you, came out of your fears (justifiably) of one sort or another...fear of harsh treatment, fear of being alone, fear of pain, and so on. Fear became the common response in your life; and it has stuck with you.

The way that we combat fear in our lives is to recognize that the opposite of fear is not courage, but love. Not love in the traditional sense, a sentiment linked to hearts and Valentine's Day, but a divine intelligence that makes up everything in the universe. As the New Testament says, "God is love." If we practice unconditional love in our lives (including unconditional love towards ourselves) by treating everything within the universe with the kindness and respect that we would have traditionally reserved for God alone, we open the channels for our heart's desires to be filled. In essence, see God in everyone and everything.

To possess this love that dispels fear, I believe you need to acknowledge a higher power at work in your life. This higher, divine power can be the power of the universe or God or whatever rings true for you. Wayne Dyer speaks eloquently of this divine love in his book *Manifest Your Destiny*. Once you acknowledge this higher power in your life and turn over control to it, you will realize, perhaps for the first time, that you are not alone in life.

Once you accept unconditional love as your outlook on life, keeping in mind that everything within the universe is connected by a divine order and intelligence, you can begin to see that you are worthy of receiving whatever good and positive things you desire. Meditate on the three ideas:

We are inseparably connected to our environment and the universe. You are worthy of the abundance of the universe and all that is in it. Unconditional love connects you to manifesting your destiny.

Please read Wayne Dyer's *Manifest Your Destiny* for further details.

*   *   *

Be Kind To Yourself

Whenever I'm having difficulty with this very important concept of unconditional love and kindness, ***I gently say, "Be kind to yourself today."*** This small statement has the power to still my racing mind and light a fire in my heart. Everything else begins to fall into place when I simply say, "Be kind to yourself today."

When you do this, overeating, overdrinking, self-doubt, self-denial, and self-abuse become unthinkably cruel acts to inflict upon yourself. Think of treating yourself like you would your dearest friend or your mother. Would you mindlessly stuff food down your mother's throat, long after she was full? Would you tell your best friend that she is not deserving of happiness or shouldn't pursue her dreams? Would you tell your dear sibling that the mean kids were right, that he or she is a stupid, lazy, fat kid? Sounds unthinkable. ***Start giving yourself the loving respect and patience you give those around you.*** Soon you will be treating the people in your life better too.

*   *   *

The Power of Changing One Thing

What one eating habit of yours is making or keeping you fat? ***Most of us have that one big, bad behavior that contributes the most to our fatness.*** I have had several at different points in my life. There was the

Bagel Finagle: an overload of bagels all day long. I ate them like some people drink diet soda or others smoke cigarettes, thinking that because they were practically fat-free, they would magically melt fat. Oh, the rides my blood sugar must have been going on!

Other popular ones from my life and their pet names include: Late Night with David and the Dinner Cleanup, Cheetos in Charge, Booze Cruise (nursing beers throughout the course of an evening), Ice Cream Hellhole (picking up some light ice cream to have around the house and finishing the quart in an evening), and Saddy Hour (when after-work happy hours turn sour).

There is tremendous power in changing just one thing in life. The impact can be astounding. Chances are you have one dark behavior that is contributing to your weight problem. Maybe it's eating off of other people's plates or frequent trips to the vending machine at work (stop and think how all those quarters add up). Spend some time thinking of what your one behavior is. Figure out a positive strategy for getting rid of it. Begin by focusing on everything else you have in your life, rather than the one behavior that is sabotaging you. Replace your big, bad behavior with one of the many positives in your life. Turn happy hour into workout time with a friend, and have a wonderful glass of wine when you get home. If you graze on junk food throughout the workday afternoon, buy yourself a hot-air popper to get you through the day. Pure resolve will not be enough. You need to have a plan in place. *Maybe your big, bad behavior is signaling a period or moment in your daily life when you need a break or need to make a change.*

*   *   *

What Are You Avoiding?

It's well worth asking yourself what you are avoiding in life by constantly turning to food. Not only does fat put the life you were born to live on hold, but also the very act of constantly eating keeps you too busy to become who you were meant to become. Realization of our true selves requires vulnerability and risk-taking. Fat and overeating keeps you from either of these. Much like a happy hour sabotages any constructive anything for the rest of the night, compulsive eating keeps you from moving forward as well.

Are you avoiding the very fact that you have a weight problem by continuing to turn to food? If you've been fat all you life, being thin probably seems like an impossibility. So much shame and self-loathing is involved with being fat that you may be mad at yourself for getting yourself to this state. Being fat can be very embarrassing. People giving you double takes, not fitting into seats, and profuse sweating are just a few of the things that draw negative attention. Living from day to day becomes an uncomfortable chore. Instead of facing your fat and your overeating, you turn to food.   As stated earlier, giving up overeating requires abandoning your best friend and greatest comforter…a scary notion. However, the comfort you receive from food is actually smothering you. Remember, if you take the first step to fulfilling your dreams, the universe will help you. God and the universe want you to fulfill your heart's desires. **Change what you know you can, and the rest will follow.**

Are you avoiding stress by turning to food? It took me a long time to learn that stress is inevitable. Learning how to manage stress is the key to not letting it (and the avoidance of it) rule us. Probably because I felt so stressed throughout my teens, I aspired to construct my life so that stress would never rear its ugly head. What I soon found out was that by eliminating stress, I was also eliminating what challenged me and ultimately brought me joy.

It's possible that you do have too much stress in your life. The key to managing stress is to make sure that the stress you are experiencing at least has a purpose in your life. If you are getting stressed over circumstances that have no real purpose, these stresses need to go away.

Are you avoiding intimacy by keeping yourself fat? Are memories of rejection by your peers scaring you into steering clear of love? You may have thoughts that you aren't worthy of love because of years of self-hatred. Concentrate on the thought that you are lovable and worthy of love exactly the way you are. The more you treat yourself in a loving way, by being kind to yourself and taking care of yourself, the more this will begin to ring true in you.

Are you avoiding career dreams and goals and focusing on food instead? Are you afraid of realizing your dreams for some reason? Does it seem self-indulgent to you? Were you raised to think that life is meant to be hard work and suffering with maybe occasional joy sprinkled in? Do you begin to pursue goals and dreams, start to feel guilty, eat to numb the guilt, and then abandon your dreams to eat some more? *Remember, following your dreams and honoring your true self is honoring the spiritual world.* It's anything but self-indulgent. Wallowing in avoidance is self-indulgent. If you take one step, the universe will honor your intention by opening up doors for you. However, you have to be willing to see the doors being opened.

Does the act of healing yourself feel like betrayal to your parents? How dare you be happier than your parents? Are we afraid of doing better than Mom and Dad? There is no "better or worse." There is only listening to your heart and honoring your own individual calling and path in life.

One sure way of uncovering what you are avoiding in life by focusing on food is to *pay close attention to your envy.* Envy arises when we see situations or circumstances that we want for ourselves and could actually see ourselves achieving, if things were only different. Do you envy thin people or people in the arts or people with successful business careers? After you've figured out what you are avoiding (trust your instincts; you are sure to be dead on) it's time to explore why you are avoiding these things. Chances are, somewhere along the line you got the idea that you weren't good enough. I swear, *show me an overweight person, and I'll show you someone who feels they aren't good enough,* not even good enough to pursue their true dreams. Some fat people channel this into a very successful life, but it may not be exactly the life that they want.

We all have kernels of unrealized dreams tucked away in ourselves. If our dreams were stunted by a reaction to an outside force, they don't just lie dormant. They infect us. They hurt and annoy us. Quite simply, they've got to get out. You don't have to do a complete 180-degree turn in your life to tend to this side of yourself. Any small amount of attention is a great start. Maybe it's time to start painting again or playing softball or playing guitar or gardening, biking, knitting, woodworking…you fill in the blank. It doesn't need to be a career change, but it very well could be. *You will feel a flood of peace and joy when you return to something wonderful that you have abandoned.* And because you've reconnected and made peace with a slice of your past, it's a joyful thing again, rather than a source of resentment. Your newly rediscovered passions will turn your focus away from mindless overeating and your preoccupation with food. It will begin to reconnect you to your true self.

*   *   *

What Do You Need?

What do you need that you are not getting that might be causing you to reach for food? I think adult fat kids are very good at not honoring what they need in life. These needs can be very simple and basic, but left ignored, they can leave enormous holes that must be filled. Eating temporarily fills the holes.

Do you need help? At work, with the house, on the computer, or with your eating? We all need help. Asking for it does not make you ignorant or a misfit. Acknowledging it and seeking out assistance is the surest step towards new growth. We can't all be experts at everything. The moment before you ask for help is the scariest. The moment after is filled with peace, hope, and confidence.

Do you need food? Sometimes we starve ourselves when we need to lose weight. This starvation triggers bingeing, which causes us to starve ourselves again and so on and so on. Are you giving yourself enough good food on a consistent basis?

Your weight problem is not a sandwich board reading "I'm lazy, weak, and unable to cope with life." Your weight problem is trying to tell you something, quite likely something that could unleash whatever is holding you back from being everything you could be. Stop blaming and begin listening to yourself. Note the times that the need to eat rises within in you. There is likely something you need at that moment or something you are avoiding that you feel you are not worthy of or is wrong.

Chapter 11

Rediscovering Your Passions in Life

How do you spend your time? For that matter, how do you view life? Is it a "have to" sort of thing for you, or do you find happiness and a sense of purpose each day?

Now that I'm halfway through my thirties, I've noticed more and more acquaintances of mine beginning to bail out on living, for lack of a better phrase. Instead of pursuing interests, trying new things, and seeking joy, they start parking themselves in front of the TV. And a large number of them are overweight. It's easy to let boredom creep into your life. ***Do you ever worry about how little activity you participate in? Have others expressed concern?***

From time to time, and certainly when we are setting out to make life changes, we need to ask ourselves, "Am I living up to my potential?" "How much joy is there in my life?" Ask yourself honestly, "How do I spend my time?" Beware of substituting how you wish you spent your time (but take note of that as well). Remember, you have the right and responsibility to enjoy your life, and anything less than that is not only a shame but also a violation of the laws of the universe.

Can you list three hobbies you actively participate in? If not, how about two? One? Do not include watching television unless what you watch accompanies another interest like old movies, cooking or tennis. So if you listed watching football, you better be playing it as well.

Hobbies say a lot about us. They tell us and others who we really are. I believe that when we are hobbying, we are at our best. A hobby is especially important if your 40-hour-a-week job is less than you would like it to be (and that you'll tackle next).

The word "hobby" can bring up images of model airplanes and stamp collecting, fine hobbies in their own right, but hobbies are far more than rainy-day activities. *Look up hobby in a thesaurus and you get phrases such as "minor obsession" and "favorite occupation."* I love that. Hobbies are good indicators of occupations you may wish to pursue if your nine-to-five job isn't everything you would hope. Hobbies are what we would do all the time, if we could. Cultivating your hobbies is important in your quest to lose weight for several reasons. *Hobbies help you define your true self.* They bring joy back into your life, and they keep you blissfully occupied and away from the kitchen (unless of course one of your hobbies is cooking). As we know, it's so easy to get our hands on food, and many of us learn to rely on food for joy, rather than looking to ourselves. Ironically, food has turned on us (or we've allowed it to), and this makes us even more depressed.

Maybe you already have hobbies, several of them even, which you love passionately. I encourage you to participate in them fully. They are worth scheduling time for. Are there ways you can bring them to a higher level of involvement or skill? If you paint, perhaps you could take a class or enter one of your paintings in an exhibit at a local art center (there are art centers in almost every community). If you garden, how about taking some gardening classes? Maybe it's time to buy a new bike. Are you an armchair quarterback? Could you spend some of your time off the couch organizing touch football games in the neighborhood or coaching pee-wee? I'm just asking you to consider the possibilities and explore the good that could come out of them. *There is tremendous potential in changing just one thing in our lives.*

What do you do if you're not sure you have any hobbies? Start with your thoughts. When you are at work, does anything besides work consume your thinking? Maybe an obsession to have the perfectly manicured, kelly-green lawn signals a potential passion for gardening. Is there anything you do in your life that you get lost in, when you lose all track of time? *Pause and consider five hobbies you would like to pursue. Write them down, in ink.*

Still having trouble? Think back to your childhood when your true self survived intact, uncensored by the real world, and the very serious act of play ruled all. *Are there hobbies you abandoned along the way because your size got in the way or because you were an outcast?* Maybe you abandoned simple things you loved over the years because you somehow got it in your head that growing up meant discarding such silliness. Rock collecting gave way to accounting.

Maybe you can develop and nurture a hobby that also involves your partner or family. Walking is a passionate activity that can be shared with others. Any resistance you may meet from those around you will dissipate if you invite without pressure or guilt. Make it your mission to explore the neighborhoods in your city, or get out of your city limits and become an expert at the park system in your area.

*   *   *

Give yourself a break!

Throughout all this talk of incorporating hobbies into our lives, *let's not forget how important it is to allow ourselves to have guilt-free idle time in our lives.* I've talked about the importance of allowing yourself breaks. For any number of reasons, not the least of which is discomfort with ourselves, we fall into the habit of grabbing food when we would rather do nothing and just be with ourselves. Then we begin to feel guilty for doing nothing (bad, lazy little fat kid), and, to numb the guilt and to do something, we eat. Dare to be idle. Allow yourself idle time. Remember, it's not wasted time if you enjoyed doing nothing.

*   *   *

Letting Hobbies into Your Life: An Action Plan

List five things you love to do, things that occupy your thoughts and make you lose track of time.

Begin in small ways (or not so small) to bring one or more of them into your life. Consider getting partners and kids involved if desired or possible.

Investigate a way to become more expert at a hobby. Check a book out of the library, visit a website or investigate a class through Open U or community education.

Acknowledge that your hobby is important. In the big scheme of life, it is possibly more important than your day job. It says most clearly who you are, and you will no doubt continue your hobby with even greater fervor once you retire.

Make your hobby, or at least a portion of it, easily accessible. Go to it when you want to eat for no good reason. A hobby corner in the basement may be just what you need.

*   *   *

Hobbies to Consider (a few of the thousands!)

Walking or running
Strength training or weight lifting
Yoga
Reading
Sports of all kinds
Drawing
Painting
Piano
Pottery
Politics
Woodworking
Ballroom dancing

History
Old movies
Bonsai
Restoring old cars
Singing (alone or in a church or community choir)
Collecting (just about anything)
Fine art and visiting museums
Photography
Bicycling

*   *   *

And another to give special consideration to…

Dogs

If you have one, you know that the phrase "man's best friend" is
not just a cliché. Greater unconditional love is difficult to find. They
are wonderful companions, a great security system for the home, and
the ultimate exercise companion…eager and nonjudgmental. If you
have a dog that is out of shape, consider it your wake-up call to exercise. Walk or run your dog every day, and you'll both lose weight.

If you don't have a dog and have the means to house one, please
consider it. I acquired Lily, a cross between some kind of terrier and a
dachshund, about a year and a half ago, and she has been a blessing.
You're never lonely with a dog in the house, but when you want to be
alone, he or she happily joins you in complete repose. I walk Lily
every day for about 30 minutes, and this has become a wind-down ritual that both of us enjoy. Being part dachshund, it's important that Lily
stay near her ideal weight (11 pounds) to avoid potential back problems. Because she's small, she fits into my small house. Kids love dogs.
And if you're searching for your life partner, walking your dog is a
great way to meet people, especially these days when a pooch on a
leash is as popular as a latte. ***Dogs nurture the soul and make wonderful companions.*** Think seriously about it.

Gardening and cooking, two more hobbies to help in your weight loss and in becoming healthier, are covered in later chapter.

Chapter 12

So…What's Up with Food?

A TV commercial ran when I was a teen that used the tines of a fork to represent the bars of a prison: cold, hard, and holding an overeater captive, helpless, and hopeless. Every time I saw this commercial I thought, "Yes, exactly." I had always felt like I was held captive by food, like it was an enemy. I had grown to hold it in the same esteem as I held the kids who made so much fun of me in junior high and the bad teachers who ignored or humiliated me in school. It possessed similar qualities to me: unreliable, untrustworthy, and a source of great shame and sadness. The bottom line was I had grown to hate food. I hated it, but I smothered myself in it…a love/hate relationship in the truest form.

Food is such a sure thing in our society; it's so easy to get our hands on. I believe that is why it has become such a common addiction. We end up pounding out any specialness it has by mindlessly shoveling it in. Pretty soon it doesn't matter how it looks or how it tastes, just as long as it's there when we need it. As I said earlier, to an overeater food can fill any or all of the following roles: pacifier, friend, enemy, lover, bully, sustainer, entertainer, comforter, tantrum-outlet, tranquilizer, upper, downer…and the list goes on. And unlike other addictions such as smoking, booze or marijuana, we have to have it. There's no going cold turkey.

Ultimately, if we want to change our eating habits and lose weight, we need to learn to live with food, to make friends with it before it kills us. This is why weight loss programs such as using protein drinks (or anything you stop using once you reach your goal weight) don't work. What do you do when you're done?

Doesn't it make sense that since we have to have food in our lives, we should embrace it, celebrate it, and turn it into a passion of ours? If we learn to hold food in high esteem, it loses its negative mystique.

*   *   *

So what does food do for us, besides make us fat?

If our bodies came with an owner's manual, there would be a huge chapter telling us exactly what food did for our bodies. Until I decided to find out, I never had a clue what it did, except make me fat and miserable, so consequently I chose to alienate myself from it. I grew to think of no food as good food, that the best choice for dinner was no dinner. It never clicked that my body needed food for basic functions and that the lack of the right kinds of food could do damage and ultimately shorten my life. I guess it takes a while for the concept of mortality to hit us. ***Also, the weird eating I was doing was actually contributing to the negative emotions that were making me eat...a vicious cycle.***

Simply put, food fuels all of our body's functions: walking, running, thinking, speaking, exercising, laughing...everything. It is our energy. Food is divided into three basic nutrient groups: carbohydrates, fats, and proteins. Nearly all whole, unrefined foods contain all three of these in varying proportions. (Yes, broccoli does have trace amounts of fat.) When the body miraculously breaks these three nutrients down, energy is released that fuels all of the aforementioned bodily functions. Food also provides us with vitamins and minerals needed for our bodily processes and gives us a large percentage of our water.

*   *   *

Each of the three nutrients serves our body in a specific way.

Protein. Protein is the only natural source of amino acids. Amino acids build and maintain muscle and help control serotonin in our brains. Serotonin is what controls our moods and makes us feel good about being alive. Protein, besides being highly satisfying, also curbs our cravings for carbohydrates. Start your day off with eggs, and you most likely won't be hungry until noon. It also helps our bodies ward off disease. When we take away the water in our bodies, the rest is nearly all protein. It makes sense that we need it daily, throughout the day.

Prime examples include:

Fowl (unfortunate name): turkey, chicken, duck, goose

Red Meat: steaks, beef roasts, hamburger, pork, ham, bacon

Fish: cod, orange roughy, flounder, trout, haddock, tuna, salmon

Shellfish: shrimp, scallops, clams, mussels

Eggs

Dairy products: milk, cheese, cottage cheese, yogurt

Soy products

Tofu (a soy product) Tofu picks up the flavor of that with which it is cooked.

Dried beans and peas (legumes)

Rice and corn (grains)

Complete proteins. The protein found in meat, dairy, and eggs is a complete protein in that it contains everything our body requires from a protein source, mainly amino acids. As far as chemical makeup goes, an animal is an animal, so cows give our bodies what we need. Soy products (including tofu) are also complete proteins...good news for vegetarians.

Incomplete proteins. Proteins from plants (other than soy products) need to be combined to form complete proteins. Dried beans or peas combined with rice or corn supplement each other to the point of providing a complete protein. Quite simply, legumes possess what grains lack, and grains possess what legumes lack. I guess that's how rice and beans became a popular combination. Corn with beans and lentils with barley are also good combinations.

Proteins also contain some amount of fats, which is good because we do need some fat. Red meat contains the most.

Fats. Fats lubricate our skin and aid crucially in digestion. Because they slow the digestion process, they are very satisfying and help keep hunger pangs at bay. They are the chief fuel for our muscles, and they also help food move through us, if you get my drift. Fats (in addition to that which is found in protein) include:

Oils: olive (the best), vegetable, corn, sunflower

Salad dressings

Mayonnaise

Butter and margarine

Carbohydrates. They are divided into simple and complex. Complex carbohydrates (veggies and whole grains) contribute significant amounts of vitamins, minerals, and fiber. They are the main fuel for our bodies. Simple carbohydrates are basically sugars and provide huge amounts of satisfaction. If we don't get enough carbohydrates, our bodies start burning protein.

Complex carbohydrates. Includes vegetables, whole grain breads, and pastas. Complex carbohydrates are basically unrefined starches. Starch breaks down easily into glucose, which is the body's primary fuel and the only fuel that the brain and central nervous system can use. Whole grains and legumes are what you could call wonder carbs in that they contain B vitamins, which the body needs to burn glucose. Plus they are a great source of protein.

Complex carbohydrates generally take longer to eat and are more texturally satisfying than other types of food. When you eat a complex carbohydrate, you really know you are eating something. They also contain fiber, which makes us feel full and helps us have regular bathroom habits.

Simple carbohydrates. Includes fruits, sugar, honey, corn syrup, molasses, desserts, sweets and goodies, and booze. Simple carbohydrates are usually very satisfying, so they do serve a purpose. People usually think of fruit as complete, but it is simple. It contains a lot of sugar, but also a lot of fiber, which helps absorb the sugar. Think of fruit as more of a treat.

*   *   *

As you probably already know, the USDA puts the basic food groups that the body needs within a day into a clever little pyramid. It's a pretty clear visual and a good way to start looking at food:

Breads, Cereal, Rice, and Pasta (6-11 servings)
Examples of one serving: 1 slice bread, small muffin or biscuit, 1/2 cup pasta or rice, 1 ounce cereal
Vegetables (3-5 servings)
Example of one serving: About a 1/2 cup of steamed carrots
Fruits (2-4 servings)
Examples of one serving: About a 1/2 cup of grapes or a medium-sized apple
Milk, Yogurt & Cheese (2-3 servings)
Examples of one serving: 1 cup milk, 1 1/3 cup cottage cheese, 1 1/2 ounces of cheese
Meat, poultry, fish, beans, eggs, and nut group (2-3 servings)
Examples of one serving: 2-3 ounces of meat (the size of your palm), 1 to 1 1/2 cups cooked peas or lentils, 2 eggs
Fats, Oils, and Simple Carbohydrates (use sparingly)
Use to accompany and enhance

I've heard a lot of buzz lately about the USDA Food Pyramid being nothing but government propaganda. There were even reports that said Food Pyramid committee members were higher-ups in the meat and dairy industries. I don't know. I still think it gives a good general guideline for daily eating.

*   *   *

Dieting

The dieting mindset makes more people fat than anything else for two reasons. First of all, the bad food vs. good food mentality guilts us into eating good foods but leaves us unsatisfied and thinking of nothing but bad foods. Because we think we can't have some foods, they hold a certain mystique and cast a type of spell over us. We try sneaking a little but feel so guilty that we sneak a little bit more. After the first candy bar, we figure we've blown our good eating for the day, so we throw in the towel and eat the whole bag of Snickers.

The second problem with the dieting mindset is the unhealthy and unnatural preoccupation with food that it creates. Measuring food down to 1/8 of a cup, sipping protein drinks, and thinking of food only in terms of calories, fats, and carbohydrates not only sterilizes it and strips it of joy but also forces the eater to give it undue attention. It's like telling a recovering alcoholic to count the bottles in a liquor store.

*   *   *

A New Relationship with Food

Begin building your new relationship with food by kicking the good food/bad food idea to the curb. One day a receptionist at work whispered to me, "There's some very, very bad cake in the lunchroom." I smiled, but I wanted to say, "Cake isn't bad. Cake is a wonderful, beautiful thing! The way we sometimes treat it is bad." All foods are fair game for your eating. You may not get all you want, but you will get them, and that fact alone can be very satisfying. *If you think of a food as bad, it probably means that only a small amount is needed to truly feel the satisfaction of the food.* Richer foods, which are generally higher in fat or sugar, satisfy us quickly.

Grab a piece of paper and list your 25 favorite foods. Think back to your childhood and remember the foods that made you happy. Pancakes and split pea soup are my childhood happy foods. Perhaps it will help you to think in terms of meals: your favorite breakfast foods, lunch foods, dinners, and snacks. Include favorites from restaurants you've visited. I've always been drawn to foods at The Mudpie, a vegetarian restaurant in Minneapolis, which led me to cook from the Mollie Katzen series of Moosewood cookbooks. Somehow, the flavors and textures speak to me, satisfy me, and make me happy. Think back to meals of special occasions as you were growing up such as Thanksgivings, birthday parties, and the like.

If you're coming up empty, let me prod your free thinking a little: cinnamon rolls, orange juice with a splash of 7-Up, banana pancakes with walnuts, cheese and mushroom omelets, homemade bread with butter and strawberry jam, grilled peanut butter sandwiches, tuna melts with sharp cheddar, Funyons, corn nuts, chips and salsa, white wedding cake with vanilla ice cream, turkey with seasoned salt, potato salad with green olives, lettuce with blue cheese dressing, and so on.

Take the exercise one step further and make a list of ten foods that you formerly thought of as bad. This is your hall of fame bad food list. This is where delights like chips and chili con queso or oatmeal pies belong. Remember, there are no bad foods. Some foods maybe shouldn't be a staple in our daily eating, but you can eat them, and they do belong in your eating plan for the satisfaction they give.

Now that you've had the fun of listing your favorite formerly bad foods, it's time to purposefully list your favorite healthier foods. Let me whisper some ideas in your ear:

Chicken Breasts Cooked in Wine and Rosemary

Roast Turkey with Whole Wheat Cranberry Stuffing

Grilled Vegetable Sandwich with Mustard on Whole Wheat Bread

Broiled Green Beans

Spinach Salad with Red Onion

Cucumbers in Vinegar Dressing

Sautéed Zucchini and Onions

Garlic Mashed Potatoes

Egg and Cheese Omelet

Fresh Steamed Asparagus

Oatmeal with a tablespoon of brown sugar

See the recipe section to learn how to make some of the above, plus more.

*   *   *

40 foods to Consider

I have a list of 40 semi-wonder healthy foods that I have made my best buddies. These foods make eating well so much easier. Some are wonders because of the good things they do for our bodies. Some I like…just because.

1. *Pure, dark chocolate.* It stimulates endorphins and boosts serotonin, which makes us feel good about being alive. A little goes a long way. I try to fit in a little bit every day. What a luxury!

2. *Salmon.* Chocked full of Omega 3 fatty acids, which allow blood to flow freely to and from the heart.

3. *Spinach.* Provides folic acid for your heart and vitamin K for your bones. Also provides fiber.

4. *Tuna.* More Omega 3, and it's so yummy, inexpensive and convenient.

5. *Oatmeal.* The soluble fiber lowers cholesterol. Add a little brown sugar, and you have a great morning treat. It's also quite filling.

6. *Blueberries.* Recently discovered to be as heart healthy as red wine.

7. *Avocado.* Absolute heaven.

8. *Garlic.* Potent and supposedly good for your heart.

9. *Air-popped popcorn.* The fiber fills you up, and the taste is kind of nutty.

10. *Broccoli.* Like its cruciferous relatives the cauliflower and cabbage, it contains indole-3 carbinols, strong cancer fighters. Anything this green has got to be good for you.

11. *Sweet Potatoes.* A cancer fighter and one of nature's sweet treats. Add a *little* butter and sugar.

12. *Tofu.* It's soybean curd. It soaks up the flavor of whatever food surrounds it and is very texturally satisfying. It provides fiber, calcium, protein (complete), B-complex vitamins, and it lowers bad cholesterol.

13. *Figs.* They give us lots of calcium, potassium, fiber, minerals and are very sweet and satisfying. You can eat them as is or add them to salads, pastas or baked goods. Fig Newtons are a gift from God.

14. *Apples.* So beautiful, full of fiber, crunchy, and sweet. When I've eaten an apple, I feel like I've really eaten something.

15. *Cucumbers.* Fresh tasting and crunchy.

16. *Red wine.* Rich in anti-oxidants (anti-oxidants neutralize free radicals which attack our body cells). It also prevents cholesterol from sticking to the walls of your arteries.

17. *Watermelon.* It's like a low-calorie, fat-free ice cream, in my book. How can anything be so sweet and so pretty and be so low in calories?

18. *Asparagus.* Folic acid for the heart. The aspartic acid makes some people's urine smell like asparagus. I know…who cares.

19. *Lentils.* Protein rich and high in fiber, they are low in fat, and they lower bad cholesterol. Combine with a grain (rice, corn or barley) to form a complete protein.

20. *Black beans.* The above goes for black beans too.

21. *Eggs.* An easy, versatile, cheap form of protein.

22. *Cantaloupe.* So low calorie and full of anti-oxidant cancer fighters.

23. *Bananas.* The potassium lowers blood pressure. The easiest fruit to tote around.

24. *Mustard.* So much flavor for so few calories. It goes with everything, including eggs.

25. *Onions.* There is something about an onion. The rich taste and slight crunchiness once again evokes images of a high-calorie food, but it's not.

26. *Cottage cheese.* Smooth, creamy, comforting, and an easy source of protein and calcium. Go for the fat-free or low-fat varieties. It doesn't affect the amount of calcium or protein.

27. *Yogurt.* A sweet treat, easy to carry around or take to work. About eight grams of protein are in eight ounces.

28. *Whole-wheat pasta.* Fiber and filling.

29. *Balsamic vinegar.* An addictive little dash and a great salad dressing.

30. *The chicken breast.* Great protein source for 200 calories.

31. *Tomato and tomato products.* Contains lycopene, a powerful anti-oxidant.

32. *Turkey.* A great protein source and seems special because of holiday memories.

33. *Dried cranberries.* Tangy and a colorful, a surprising addition to many things.

34. *Brown rice.* Good fiber and chewy.

35. *Mushrooms.* A lot of taste for almost no calories.

36. *Green beans.* A veggie wonder with great color.

37. *Soy nuts.* 10 grams of protein and plenty of crunchiness in one ounce.

38. *Whole-wheat bread.* All you need is one slice of a really good bread. You get fiber, a little protein, and a full tummy.

39. *Really good coffee.* Coffee raises your metabolism (two cups a day will raise your metabolism enough to burn 200 calories), and it gives you a little jolt when you need it. If you like coffee, you love cof-

fee. Coffee drinkers know what I mean. Treat yourself to the good stuff. Get yourself a grinder, and buy the whole beans…and don't be skimpy when you brew your own. And when you are out and about, treat yourself to a stop at a coffeehouse instead of cookies, candy or what have you.

40. Herbal teas. A sweet, soothing way to end your day.

*   *   *

Calories?

Yes, they do count, but you don't need to count them one by one. Learning to listen to yourself about what kind and how much food you want and to use a visual approach to eating (explained later) is a much easier, joyful, and equally effective way to keep track. **Ask yourself, "Is what I'm about to eat going to nourish and supplement my body or give me great satisfaction?"** If not, move on to something that will.

Now, having said that, it's helpful to understand what a calorie is and the role it plays in running our bodies and maintaining our weight. A calorie is simply a means of measuring the amount of heat or fuel that food supplies to the body. If more calories are consumed than are burned, the calories are stored as fat for later use. Sounds kind of positive when you think of it that way, but, unfortunately, the means of storage (fat) isn't particularly attractive. A little stored fat isn't too bad, but too much is unhealthy, needless to say.

Generally speaking, about 1,500 calories for women and 2,000 for men are good, safe numbers to shoot for to lose weight. I had become so out of touch with my natural eating, I didn't even know what 2,000 calories in a day looked like. The idea is to pay close attention to what we really want to eat to help us determine a good amount of daily calories, but I think looking at what a 1,500 or 1,800 or 2,000-calorie day consists of helps to put it all in perspective.

A Sample 1,800-calorie day

Oatmeal, 1/2 cup, dry	200 calories
1 cup skim milk	90
1 tsp. brown sugar	25
Tub of yogurt	80
Tuna Sandwich	
2 slices whole wheat bread	160
1 can of tuna	150
Tablespoon light mayonnaise	65
Orange	65
Apple	80
1/2 cup cottage cheese	80
Chicken breast	200
Potato	100
2 cups of green veggies	50
1/2 tsp. margarine	50
2 cups spinach	30
1/4 cup chopped onion	15
2 tablespoons light	
salad dressing	40
2 glasses white wine	320
Total	**1,800**

1,500-calorie day

From the 1,800-calorie day, subtract one wine (160 calories), half the oatmeal (100 calories) at breakfast and substitute balsamic vinegar for the salad dressing (40 calories) at dinner.

2,000-calorie day

To the 1,800-calorie day, add 1/4 cup of almonds (200 calories) for your dinner salad and to snack on.

2,200-calorie day

To the 1,800-calorie day, add 1/4 cup almonds (200 calories) and two chocolate chip cookies (200 calories).

*   *   *

What do I eat in a day? The Visual Approach

I previously listed the components of the USDA food group pyramid to give you an idea of what your body needs in a day. If you are smaller framed, go to the lower number; if you're bigger, go to the higher number. The intent is to make your eating an easy, natural, and joyous experience. Begin thinking of your plate of food in visual terms rather than in cups and ounces. Your plate at each meal should be divided into thirds: one third protein, one third carbohydrates, and one third additional green leafies.

Protein. We all need about 20 to 25 grams, three times a day. *The appropriate size of your protein portion is pretty easy to eyeball. It's about the size of the palm of your hand* or a computer mouse or a can of tuna. This is the basis from which you determine your carbohydrates and your additional green leafies. *Aim for making your complex carbohydrates about the size of your protein and your green leafies at least that size.* If you get more than your palm-size worth of protein in a restaurant (and most of the time you will), that's what goes in a doggy bag, and guess what? You're the lucky doggie. Leftovers will taste great in an omelet the next morning.

Carbohydrates. *Match your complex carbohydrates to your protein.* Whole wheat is always the best choice and, quite honestly, the most flavorful and texturally satisfying. Try to get in the mindset that the grainier it is, the better. If you have dessert, cut down on the carbohydrates during the meal.

Additional Green Leafies. Learn to love green leafies. Learn to love them a lot. As a matter of fact, make them your best friend or a second spouse to follow you though life. You may be haunted by memories of pale, rubbery canned beans and yellow iceberg lettuce with sugary, goopy salad dressings. It's time for your green leafies to grow up. And to go with our visual approach to eating, the more vivid the color, the better it is for you. Green leafies give you mega doses of vitamins and minerals, lots of good roughage, and cancer-fighting anti-oxidants. *You need to shoot for about 4 cups a day.* Plus, green leafies make a beautiful plate. My mom always commented on the splendid color composition or occasional blah-ness of her dinners with "Oooh, I'd get an A in Home Ec. class for this plate." Grilled green beans with walnuts in olive oil and spinach salads with feta cheese, onions, and almonds are in your future.

Snacks. I like to think of them as food rituals. Not sick, twisted, idiosyncratic bents, but little traditions that I have set up for myself throughout the course of the day to sustain myself physically and emotionally. If you are eating enough protein, 20 or so grams three times a day, spaced out equally, you won't need much of a snack, or at least your body won't. Your mind may. *It helps some folks to spread their three meals out into six little meals throughout the day.* It helps keep hunger at bay, keeps your metabolism burning fat, and gives you a little treat to look forward to…often.

*   *   *

Make Sure You Have Food Around

You simply must make sure you have good food in the house, at work or wherever you spend a lot of time. It won't guarantee you are going to eat it, but it sure ups the chances. You've made your list of favorite, healthy foods. You've seen my list. Set yourself up for success by having these foods on hand. When you're scattered and stressed at work and find yourself staring at the box of day-old donuts in the lunchroom, go make yourself some popcorn or eat your tuna sandwich a little early or have a yogurt and small piece of chocolate in the afternoon.

If all you want to do on a Sunday afternoon at home is eat, remember how much you love sweet potatoes. Bake yourself one and have it with a pat of butter. Eat some turkey. Make yourself a big plate of green beans. Have a dish of pasta. Make a cup of great coffee. Give yourself something you love that is good for you when you want to eat. Be sure you have the good stuff on hand.

Also, you need to plan your eating to a point, especially at the beginning of your new way of eating. Make notes for yourself if you like or just keep mental notes. Have a rough idea of what you are going to eat each day.

*   *   *

The Need for Snacks

As just mentioned, undereating at meals can cause a yearning for snacks. As fat people and dieters, we sometimes get it into our heads that we don't have a right to eat. You have the right to make each meal an event, a nourishing event. And protein will keep your belly quiet. Yet, even if we eat enough at meals, other factors can trigger us to snack. They include:

Not finding passionate work or passionate pastimes to fill our day. This leaves us restless and searching for food when we are idle or bored.

Not allowing ourselves to take breaks. How often do you let yourself check out? I'll bet a lot less than you initially think. Next time you feel an urge to eat at work or at home, ask yourself if you just need a break. Stress, confusion, and anger are natural, expected human emotions that will pass, which leads to the next point.

Not feeling your feeling. Get mad; then get over it. I challenge you. Feel the feeling, and you won't want a treat.

Now, if you really want a snack (and that's fine), protein, complex-carbo, and green leafy snacks are the best snacks. The best thing to come out of the protein craze and carbo-addict information overload is a green light to eat meat and to dress our green leafies with dressings we like.

*   *   *

Not eating after 8 p.m.

Oh my God, will this make a difference in your weight loss! Everything you eat after 8 p.m. does not get burned up by your body and just sits there as unused energy turning into fat. Officially close the kitchen after 8 p.m. Move to another room for the night. Brush your teeth. Dream and fantasize about what you'll eat tomorrow. Walk. Do anything. If you can detour the late night graze, you will see the difference it makes. Trust me here.

*   *   *

Beer, Wine and Spirits

So what's the deal with booze and losing weight? We've all heard the buzz on alcoholic beverages and how they fit into a healthy eating plan. Generally speaking, they don't all that well. In my experience, the proportionately high calorie content in cocktails is the least negative effect. ***More adverse is the magical ability alcohol has to kill your good intentions.***

A couple of drinks relax you. The feeling is good, very calming, and temporarily you are very happy and peaceful. You don't want the feeling to go away, so you have another. Something kicks in somewhere between your taste buds and your brain, and suddenly salty pretzels or tortilla chips are calling out to you. Their crunchiness seems to go hand in hand with your drinks. Somehow the snacks complete the party picture. Your inhibitions are squelched from the liquor, and you either forget that you have a new way of eating, or you plan to have just a few chips. A basket or two later you decide that this was your last hurrah; tomorrow everything will suddenly be better, and you'll never party again. I've had periods in my life when too much drinking was my one great behavior keeping me from losing weight. It was amazing to see what a difference cutting my alcohol consumption in half did to my weight loss efforts. Oprah Winfrey recommends doing the "cut-in-half" approach to drinking in her book *Make the Connection*.

Undeniably, alcohol is high in calories. The approximate calorie counts of a few favorites are as follows:

Red or White Wine, average-sized glass (7 oz.) 160 calories

Beer, Pilsner glass (14 oz.) 176 calories

Margarita, small to medium-sized glass (7 oz.) 250 calories

Martini, large-sized, stiff (5 oz.) 300 calories

Shots of Hard Liquor: rum, gin, brandy, vodka, whiskey (3 oz.) 200 calories

So we are looking at roughly 200 calories a cocktail…and most people don't stick to just one.

If you enjoy drinking, you can fit it into your healthy eating plan. It just needs to be viewed as a pleasurable indulgence, not a bad food. Like desserts or other rich foods, less alcohol is required to really feel satisfied. If you have drinks during the course of a day, hopefully after 5 p.m., treat them like desserts, and eat fewer carbohydrates at the closest meal. But care must be taken with alcohol, like with desserts and other sweets. If we view alcohol as a bad thing, that we are sneaking it into our eating and we will never have it again, a binge or over-indulgence is likely. Remember, you can have a drink tomorrow and the next day and the next day. If you keep this in mind, sticking to a drink or two is easier.

Drinking what you really want to drink, versus what's cheap or what seems less bad, will also keep you from over-indulging. If you order what you really want and allow yourself to really taste what you are drinking, you will be ten times more satisfied than if you ordered the cheap light beer or bar pour rum and diet cola. *Also, you've probably noticed that only the first two drinks taste good. After that they taste bitter, sour or somewhat acidic.* After two drinks the enjoyment is gone, and the alcohol becomes just mind-numbing empty calories. If you drink water along with your drinks, your drinks will last longer, and you'll help fight the dehydrating qualities of alcohol. Don't quench your thirst with alcohol. Do that with water.

I love the term "spirits" when referring to alcohol; it captures the true spirit of drinking. Drinking should be savored and used to add spice to celebrations. It also helps bring out the flavor in certain foods. A crisp white wine plays perfectly off a savory grilled chicken breast, and red wine is a wonderfully decadent companion to a piece of chocolate.

I do not profess to be an expert on alcoholism, but I do think people who battle with overeating are prone to what I call drinking ruts, drinking too much for stretches of time, usually not enough to be out of control, but just enough to zap energy and focus. A lot of the comfort that food temporarily offers can also be found in alcohol. Plus, if you are drawn to sweets, liquor has the same general chemical makeup. If you limit your drinking to what you really want and do so with the mindset that you can have more tomorrow or the next weekend, you will be less prone to abusing it. Also, admit that having more than a couple drinks a day can be harmful to your liver and to your overall functioning as a human being. With this in mind, you simply have to find tactics for moderation.

*   *   *

Water

Become an avid water drinker. Besides being generally good for your body, it helps weight loss in several ways. First, it must be said that since we are about 60% water, it only makes sense to incorporate the drinking of it into our lives. Rehydrate yourself first thing in the morning with a big glass. It's been at least eight hours since your body has had some. Keep a covered sippy bottle of it by your side at work and when you exercise, and keep a glass nearby while you putter around the house.

Water is crucial in digestion and maintaining the good health of your internal organs. It also keeps your skin moisturized. If you haven't been much of a water drinker in the past, once you begin incorporating it into your life you will notice your skin become more naturally smooth and soft.

Because it contains minerals, water does raise your metabolism. It helps keep you from retaining water by acting as a natural diuretic. The more you drink, the less extra water you will retain. Plus, you'll be more regular as it helps food move through your body more quickly and easily. Water can help you feel full between meals, and drinking it at meals will slow down your eating pace and make you feel full sooner...and it will keep your mouth occupied if you feel like overeating.

Now, I have no medical basis for this, but I know from personal experience that **even mild dehydration causes me to be slightly depressed and disoriented.** I've noticed on days when I just can't quite get my act together, maybe I'm having trouble focusing on one thing or I'm feeling a little blue, if I have a glass or two of water, I feel much better. It's a sure pick-me-up, like nature's Prozac. When I start the day with a big glass of water, I have a brighter, more focused day, and I feel more optimistic.

We are told to drink about two quarts (64 oz.) of water each day (more if we're sweating a lot). Personally, I would at least double that.

Part III

Moving On…

Chapter 13

Becoming Passionate About Food

As mentioned earlier, doesn't it make sense that since we must have food in our lives, we should learn to embrace it, celebrate it, and develop it into a passion? I encourage you to explore the world of food. **If you need to learn something, become an expert on the subject.** What an empowering idea, and, goodness knows, when it comes to food, the resources are everywhere. **If you learn to love the magic of food, it is my belief that you will be much less likely to abuse it.** If you know food inside and out, you are no longer helpless to its powers.

Being skilled in the kitchen is very hot right now, and for you macho guys out there, it's very manly (take Emeril LeGasse, Bobby Flay, and Ming Tsai). Cooks are held in high esteem in most every society and are considered to be nurturing, creative, charismatic, and inventive sorts.

Cooking is a wonderful pastime, hobby or passion, and I can guarantee you, if you investigate it as an art form, you will look incredibly forward to doing it and will find endless hours of joy in the kitchen. **So many wonderful, life-affirming activities involve cooking.** It's a wonderful way to entertain your friends and family, it's a great way to meet and get to know people better, and it's a fun activity for a date. Nothing could be more expressive. I think that's why almost every artist I know (painters, potters, actors and musicians) is drawn to cooking.

I've talked about the importance of developing pastimes and passions when battling weight issues. Cooking gives you all the benefits of a pastime or hobby. It reduces stress, and it's something to do when you're bored. It doesn't have to be mealtime to cook. You can make bread for dinner, chop vegetables to have on hand or bake cookies (if you have the constitution to have them in the house). You probably already have nearly everything you need to start, and, once again, you've got to eat.

*   *   *

Kitchen Facelift

Chances are your kitchen could probably use a makeover. Even if it is well equipped and organized, you may never have looked at it as a creative place where you would want to spend a lot of time.

Maybe a paint job would be just what your kitchen needs to inspire the creative chef in you. Red is a passionate color and is said to inspire creativity. If that is a little bold for you, try yellow to incite positive energy or blue for peace. Think back to your childhood. Is there a color that brings back fond memories? I painted my kitchen Martha Stewart's Batter Bowl Green because the shade reminded me of my grandma's huge kitchen that always seemed so warm, inventive, and aromatic. Most kitchens can be painted with two gallons of paint, so for $40 you can have a whole new kitchen.

Look for artwork or interesting sculptural pieces to hang in your new creative space that inspire you or make you happy. Is there a print that celebrates the joy of food? The French food advertisement prints that are so hot right now certainly do. And you don't need to spend a lot of money. Clip interesting ads or personally inspiring images out of magazines and frame them to hang in your cooking space. Instant art.

Or would you like to collect old eggbeaters and hang them on the wall? Do you have something from your grandma to display? My grandma's cooking awards above my sink inspire me to continue learning more about food and cooking. I framed and hung an apron with the Two Fat Ladies on it, which was a gift from a friend. It reminds me of the joy I have had cooking for my friends and also celebrates the joy the Two Fat Ladies seem to get from cooking with the foods they love. Plus, Jennifer (the dark haired lady) reminds me of my mother.

I recommend getting a radio or CD/tape player for your kitchen. Music adds incredibly to the experience of cooking and eating by adding an additional sensory experience, and it allows you to mount your own little creative productions in the kitchen. A TV can be a great addition as well, especially if you have cable TV and can tune into the Food Network while you work in the kitchen.

You are reinventing your relationship with food. The kitchen is no longer just another room in the house. It's a creative place, a sacred place, and a place for inspiration. Once you have your physical surroundings as you wish, you need to seek out resources to get your creative juices flowing. At the end of this book, I've included many of my favorite recipes to help you get started, but please don't stop there. As mentioned earlier, nothing beats the Food Network for inspiration. It's like having a continuous cooking class in your house. Seeing these experts manipulate food and witnessing the joy they get from the process is inspiring, and it is exactly what I am encouraging you to do.

Magazines are another accessible means of inspiration and recipes. Also, their detailed layouts make them wonderful teaching tools. My favorites are *Bon Appetit* (a must have with special sections on 30-minute meals and healthy eating) and *Cooking Light* (the name says it all). Check out the Taste or Food section of your local paper as well. The Taste section of the *Minneapolis Star and Tribune* covers cooking basics, seasonal fare, and recipes from great area restaurants…a wonderful and inspiring resource.

You will want to start investing in some cookbooks. Start off with one great one. An excellent basic one is *Better Homes and Gardens New Cookbook*. It has every classic recipe you could imagine. It also shows fundamental techniques, which are very helpful but also great fun to learn (and you are a student of cooking now). Check thrift stores and half price bookstores for this one. I see it all the time, everywhere for less.

Some of my other favorites include *The Moosewood Cookbook; The Enchanted Broccoli Forest; Eat More, Weigh Less; Laurel's Kitchen;* and the *New Basics Cookbook*. Also, don't overlook your mother's church cookbook. The fare found in these little gems is probably more for treats and special occasions, but they have yummy little treasures within their covers. Plus, they allow us to recreate good memories of foods from times that maybe weren't so happy. The food from our childhood was good food. We may just have bad memories linked to it.

When you have the bones of your kitchen looking the way you'd like, you'll want to attack the guts. **Keep in mind that your kitchen now has a great, new purpose. It houses your new passion, and it helps you create healthy, nutritious, and enjoyable food for your body.** Get rid of anything that doesn't serve this purpose. If it's ugly, remove it. Move knick-knacks that have sentimental value to high shelves to make room for working on the countertops. And clean the oven.

*   *   *

The Pantry

The objective here is to have only items that you need. Any food that you have no intention or desire to use, donate to a food shelf or throw away. A well-stocked, healthy-eater, food-lover's pantry includes:

Olive oil. It's been found to contain anti-oxidants (cancer fighters), and it has a positive effect on your cholesterol level, making it healthy for your heart. It's also delicious.

Non-stick cooking spray. Use it when oil isn't in order...makes cleaning up easier too.

A pepper mill. Fresh, cracked pepper is a delight to the palette and more potent than the pre-ground pepper in the canister.

Vinegar. It is great for salad dressings or as a flavor in many things.

Nuts. They add so much to so many recipes. When in doubt, try a little in a recipe. Roasting them in a pie tin under the broiler for a few minutes brings out the flavor. Salads are better with them, and a handful here and there gives you a nice dose of B vitamins and some protein. Use unsalted ones, please, or your ankles will puff.

Spices and Herbs. They are the color in your cooking. Explore them, research them, clip articles and paste them in the inside of cupboards. Do whatever you need to do, but get them into your life. Use of spices elevates you to a higher level of cooking. My favorites include:

Basil. This is the must-have herb in my opinion. Grow it in containers or in your garden. It's great in anything, really, but especially in tomato-based sauces and dishes. And pesto is a gift from God! (see recipes)

Bay laurel. Buy the leaves or grow a tree as a houseplant. It adds a wonderful, rich aroma to any stew or roast or soup. Be sure to remove from dishes before serving. One leaf can choke you if swallowed.

Cilantro. It's so cheap in the store and very easy to grow. Its fresh taste is welcome in salads, salsa, and poultry. Experiment a lot with this one.

Chives. This is another must-have in everyone's lawn or garden. Add fresh just before serving to eggs, potatoes, and salads.

Nasturtium. It's so easy to grow. It doesn't add much flavor, but this edible flower will add a visual wow to anything you cook. It makes cooking fun.

Oregano. It's a potent, crucial addition to chicken and sauces.

Parsley. This is great in salads or tossed with baby potatoes or sprinkled on whole-wheat pasta. It also freshens breath and takes excess water out of your body.

Rosemary. You've got to have it. It reinvents chicken and pizzas. Grow your own plant to save money.

Fresh garlic. It adds to almost anything. Chopped garlic in the jar is a great second choice.

*   *   *

The Fridge...Mother of the Kitchen

Filtered Water Pitcher. Water is so much better and better for you when filtered, and filters are so inexpensive these days that everyone can have one. The filter on the faucet is also a good option and only a little more expensive up front. Grab your water bottle and carry it around. Check into a water filter at work. It costs about $20 a month for a service, and clients and customers love it. Everybody's drinking water these days, and water from a tap can taste a little off.

The Deli Drawer. Use it for your array of great cheeses like: Swiss, Gruyere, havarti, provolone...the list is endless. Pop a piece for quick protein and calcium, and do yourself, your friends, and family a favor by trying the different ones. They may seem a bit spendy, but you'll be amazed at how a little dab will do you.

Keep some easy-to-eat meat here too. I've started a ritual of roasting a turkey, cutting it up into thirds, freezing two of the thirds, and keeping one third in the deli drawer. You can use this for cooking, sandwiches (on whole wheat bread, please) or, best yet, a quick snack here and there. If I crave chips or a cookie as I walk through the kitchen, I grab a little turkey. A protein snack gives you greater satisfaction and more nutrition than a carbo snack. Have it with a green leafy, and you will also get some fiber.

Eggs. They're an easy, cheap, protein-rich breakfast, but don't keep them in the holes provided in older fridges...not a constant enough temperature, especially if you have kids and teens frequently opening the door.

Crispers. You know, those drawers at the bottom of the fridge. They're more than just a coffin for dead fruit. They're the new home for your green leafies. Remember, your new best friend? Try to get in the habit of going there first when you open the fridge. It helps to wash your produce when you get home from the grocery store and put it in the crisper, ready to eat when you need it.

Salad dressings. The best piece of dieting news I've heard in a long time is the acceptance of regular (not the fat free) salad dressings. The fat free sorts contain added sugar, and the fat in the regular varieties helps our bodies absorb the nutrients in the veggies. Suddenly, veggies and a little of your favorite dressing (let's hear it for blue cheese, ranch, and 1,000 Island) are a great snack. The taste is ten times as great. Try balsamic vinegar as a dressing as well.

Mustard. For so few calories, fat, and carbohydrates, mustard offers such a mega-dose of taste.

Salsa. Not only is it great with baked chips, but it is also wonderful on an omelet, as a meat marinade and even as a veggie dip.

*　　　　　*　　　　　*

Your Kitchen Hardware

The secret, I believe, to good kitchen hardware (the pots and pans, utensils, and bake ware) is to have select, top-notch pieces in great condition. It will make cooking easier and much more pleasurable. Some great ones to have include:

A sauté pan with Teflon. It is perfect for omelets and sautéing your veggies. Remember, oil is not an enemy, but you can also sauté in a little water or chicken broth. Teflon is the healthy eater's friend, but throw it out when the Teflon becomes furry. You'll know what I mean when it gets to that point. Make sure you have the right utensils to not scratch your pans. (Look for my Crystal Light chicken in the recipe section.)

A mini-broiler pan. Use this for grilling a few chicken breasts or pork chops without firing up the big broiler pan. It's easier to clean up too.

A chicken cone. This is a nifty, cheap little tool that you insert into the posterior of a chicken and set in a pan to roast a chicken while allowing all the excess fat to drip into the pan.

A steamer basket. It's a nifty little metal basket that sets inside a saucepan. You place your veggies in the basket, fill the saucepan with water up to the bottom of the basket, and boil your water with the cover on the saucepan. You may want a big steamer with a large basket, but this little contraption is easy to set up and easy to clean. Plus, you can pick one up for a couple bucks in any utensil aisle of Target or your grocery store.

An air-bake cookie sheet. It's just a great cookie sheet to have.

A jelly-roll pan. This works well for broiling green beans (see recipe section).

A good quality, sharp knife. If you've never had one, it will be an epiphany for you. Mortgage the kids for one. It will make the difference between heaven and hell in the kitchen.

A kitchen scissors. This small investment gives huge returns. Makes cutting up chicken and herbs a breeze. You'll find countless uses.

Food dehydrator. They're so inexpensive these days and go hand in hand with gardening and growing your own veggies. You can dry 'til your heart's content to stock up on herbs for the winter.

Blender. Fruit smoothies are a sweet, healthy indulgence. Start with two cups of ice (a blender with an ice chopping setting is a blessing. I crush mine in a hand-operated crusher), a splash of skim milk or yogurt, and whatever fruit you wish. Banana smoothies are my favorite.

Food processor. This becomes invaluable once you start cooking more. It can easily chop your vegetables for you, and it's great for making pesto and other dishes.

A good coffee maker and coffee grinder. Good coffee can be as satisfying as a chocolate dessert. Well, almost. Grinding your own beans, if you've never done it, opens up a whole new world of taste. An espresso maker (very reasonably priced these days) is also a great idea. Decaf lattes with skim milk after dinner are a real treat.

Tea kettle. If you're not a coffee drinker, or even if you are, the world of tea is worth investigating, especially the land of naturally sweet herb teas.

Hot air popcorn popper. The popcorn almost has a roasted taste to it. You can fill up for about 200 calories with no fat. I confess that I sneak it into the movie theatres. When theatres start offering it, I will stop.

A chair. If you don't have an eat-in kitchen, put a chair or stepstool in it. It's amazing what a place for you or a cooking partner to sit will do to the atmosphere of the kitchen. Suddenly the kitchen is a welcoming place, a destination, rather than just a pass-through.

*   *   *

Steps to committing yourself to being a great cook:

Cook with patience. Cooking is not a hasty art form. Many recipes have only a few steps, but, generally speaking, if you find yourself rushing, something will go wrong.

Try a new recipe, no matter how simple, every week. However, challenge yourself to a more complicated one at least once a month. Only by trying the more advanced do you learn the techniques of the professionals. Also, though I break this rule, I don't recommend making something the first time when you have guests coming over. Spare yourself the pressure.

Start with something familiar, maybe something your mother or father made or something you saw on TV.

Make events out of your new hobby. Cook Sunday night dinner (a great way to avoid the Sunday night blues) and invite the family. Make it special. Welcome them to your new passion.

I really do believe that if someone doesn't like to cook, it only means they haven't given it enough of a chance. It's so calming, creative, and nurturing. It can do wonders for anyone. If you hesitate, start out small. Make a side dish for a store-bought roasted chicken. Try an appetizer for Sunday supper. Bake an angel food cake. Clean up as you go. A kitchen filled with dirty dishes at the end of your adventure could kill the spirit in anyone.

Chapter 14

The Best Exercise is Pushing Yourself Away from the Table

My mother always said it. I understand what she meant, especially when I look back at all the years when I was using exercise merely to counter the tons of food I was eating. I think what she was really trying to say is that the best way to lose weight is to strike a healthy balance between eating and exercise. Up until my mid-twenties, I viewed exercise as something extreme and difficult that had to be done in Olympic proportions if it was to do any good at all. This was probably because of the enormous amounts of food I was consuming. I would have had to run marathons to lose weight.

The concept of exercise may overwhelm you, especially if you grew up overweight. Exercise conjures up images of nightmarish phy. ed. classes, being picked last for the team, and feeling uncomfortable in the shorts and T-shirt you were made to wear. Also, most of us who grew up as fatties feel so disconnected from our bodies. We can't imagine being able to do any form of physical activity with any amount of grace, skill, confidence, comfort or success. Running, biking, and roller-skating were left behind with the other abandoned dreams of a fat child.

Chances are if you are overweight to the point that you feel very uncomfortable with your body, you may have the most success starting with solo forms of exercise. The good news is you can have the body you envision without worrying about being picked on or picked for the team or fitting into a gym-suit. ***Plus, the reasons for adding exercise to your life are numerous.***

As you've heard and read over and over, exercise speeds weight loss by raising your metabolism and by burning calories. If you do it regularly (at least three times a week) you will notice the difference. I guarantee you. If you do it more, you will really notice the difference. It joyfully occupies your time and will give you another passionate hobby on which to focus your attentions.

Exercise will make you stronger. Once you've dropped a few pounds, you will even see the muscles develop, and nothing is more encouraging than to see the ripple of a muscle. ***You will have visible proof that you do have control over your body.***

It clears your head and elevates your mood. This is a biological fact. Exercise releases endorphins, which results in a natural high. Focus on that fact when you're having trouble getting yourself off the couch. It will help you live longer, which, once you begin getting in touch with your true self, will become an increasingly more appealing notion to you.

Exercise helps us connect to a part of ourselves which we may have abandoned long ago... the kid who delights in play and physical activity and has the confidence to try anything. I never roller skated as a child. I was too fat to feel comfortable trying, and, besides, I didn't have any friends with whom to go. Recently I knew I wanted to try a new form of exercise. I have always admired in-line skaters, the grace and dance-like rhythm they employ. Plus, their legs look fabulous. In-line skaters seem content and peaceful when they're skating.

I couldn't imagine myself ever being able to in-line skate until I went to an ice-skating show that my niece was in. A friend made the point that the only difference between the kids and me was that they hadn't learned to be afraid and to think that they couldn't do it. Armed with that thought and all the protective gear possible, I tried it.

The first five minutes I wanted to give it up, but I set the goal of skating up and down my front sidewalk (about 20 feet) for half an hour, and I did it. This gave me enough of the feel to venture down to the main sidewalk where I made it my goal to skate back and forth for fifteen minutes. Within an hour I had progressed enough (bad knees and all) to know I could do it.

I can't impress upon you enough the battle I had to wage in my own head to think that I could even attempt to in-line skate. Never having roller skated or ice skated and never having participated in many things physical throughout my life, I had no confidence that I could do it. You may be feeling the same way about any form of exercise, but I assure you, the barriers are in your head. You may need to start small and slow, but small steps in a beginner make as much of a difference as large steps in the more experienced. Break your big goal into small goals. It works.

The best exercise for you is the one that you will do. I see friends of mine who are on their second or third membership at the local health clubs. They don't go, but the $40 still gets sucked out of their checking accounts every month. On some level, they want fitness and health in their lives, but something is not clicking.

Even though this book is not based on rules of conduct, there are a few hard and fast rules that you need to accept. One of those hard and fasts is that to lose weight and live a healthy life, **you need to incorporate exercise into your life.**

Now, I'd like to once again state that **the secret to successfully incorporating exercise into your life is finding an exercise that you will enjoy.** It is important to remember (and this is where a lot of folks falter) that it often takes at least a couple weeks to see or even feel the benefits of an exercise activity. I've seen a lot of friends give up just when they were about to turn the corner.

*   *   *

Find something you will do...

Ask yourself if there was anything you loved to do as a child that was abandoned for whatever reason. Was it dancing, skating, walking in the woods or running? It will do your spirit and self-confidence wonders to recover it.

Is there anything for which you have a knack? If you are drawn to water and feel at home in it, swimming at the YMCA may be your thing. Don't censor yourself when you explore this question. A knack can be as little of a thing as having done it once and having enjoyed it.

And speaking of enjoying, what do you enjoy doing? It's your best bet for fitness. Jazzercise was a turning point for me. Finding something that was enjoyable and good exercise was a dream come true. Even if your favorite exercise doesn't seem like a strenuous one, daily moderate exercise will do as well for you, if not better, than a strenuous activity a couple times a week. Plus, it feeds your soul and your psyche because you enjoy it.

Does your geographic location or climate suggest options to you? I live in an architecturally rich area of Minneapolis. Walking the neighborhoods is a visual treat and an architectural history lesson at the same time. If I lived near the ocean, I would certainly come up with an exercise that could be done along the seashore, such as running. Also, because I live in a state that has snow on the ground at least one third of the year, ice skating is on my list of exercises to try next.

What will fit into your lifestyle everyday? Even if you don't do it every day, you should shoot for activities that have the capacity to be incorporated into your daily life. If there is a gym between work and home, that may be the answer. Gyms aren't for everyone, but they do offer everything the fitness-minded would ever need. Also, if you are motivated by seeing others work towards their fitness goals, like "we're all in this together," gyms are for you.

If someone would have told me a year ago that I would soon belong to a gym, I would have said that he or she were crazy. I never thought a gym was for me. I saw myself as too much of a loner and too cheap.

Well, I joined, and it has been a turning point, especially in getting rid of those last few pounds. A gym has everything you would ever need for your exercise regime, plus new things to try all the time. I wanted to start lifting weights to build my upper body strength and, to be quite honest, look better. The machines that the gyms have for weight lifting make it easier and safer for beginners.

I thought I would go crazy surrounded by others at the gym, but I put on my walkman when I lift weights and read my magazine on the cross-trainer, and it's a wonderfully relaxing and quite spiritually uplifting alone time for me. I feel like I'm doing a wonderful thing for me, and I am. Because I live in a cold climate, being able to go to the gym in the cold winter months, work up a sweat, move my body, and relax in the sauna and hot tub is therapy. And because I'm going somewhere to exercise, I actually schedule the time.

What made me go? I received a coupon in the mail for a free visit to Bally's Lifetime Fitness, and, on a rainy afternoon, I figured it would at least be a good way to get in some exercise. I received a very high-pressure sales pitch at first (I can't blame them; they have to make a living too), but I also received a free session with a personal trainer. The aerobic exercises felt good (the cross-trainer and the stair climber), but what made me really think twice about the gym was the feeling I got from lifting the weights. There was definitely an adrenaline rush as I lifted. *I could also specifically feel my individual muscles as I worked them, which is very empowering and encouraging. To feel the burn in specific muscles being worked gave me the clear picture that I had control over shaping my body to the way that I wanted.* I had also been doing only aerobic exercise for so long (walking mainly) that I needed a change or at least the addition of something new. Plus, it felt good to be at the gym, like I was investing some solid time and energy in my well-being. Quite simply, it was a very positive experience.

I didn't join the Bally's. I joined the YMCA. After the Bally's visit I asked for a free visit at the nearby Y (I think any club will give you this). *My reasons for joining the Y highlight the main points to consider when choosing a gym or health club.*

Location. Location. Location. I firmly believe that the club has to be very accessible to you. You need to determine what is convenient, but, for me, anything over a 15-minute commute would deter my going. If you work outside the home, a club that is between home and work is perfect. Just think of it as stopping off for some unwinding time after work.

The general feel and tone of the club. Clubs seem to be either beautiful-people clubs or gym-like. I prefer the gym-like atmosphere. That is why I chose the Y over Bally's. Make sure to test drive several clubs and take careful note of your comfort level while at the club. This is a rather indefinable but crucial point. Generally, the more people like you that there are at the club, the more comfortable you will be, and if you're not comfortable, you will not go.

Cleanliness. You may not be a neat freak, but a dirty club is just a downer and not at all conducive to making positive changes in your life. A good club will be very dedicated to cleanliness. By nature of what's going on there, a club is like a greenhouse for germs and bacteria. If the club is dirty when you visit, don't think that it is just an off day. Keep looking. I can't stress this small but important point enough.

Options. The club should have more options than you would ever think in your wildest dreams you would ever need. You may not engage in yoga or power-lifting or pilates or running on a treadmill or use a personal trainer or attend nutrition classes or kick box or use a cross-training machine, but as you become more in touch with your physical self, you will develop the confidence and enthusiasm to try new things.

*   *   *

Accessible Forms of Exercise

Walking—An Overweight Person's Best Friend. I would highly recommend walking to everyone. I believe it has life-changing powers. If you are very overweight and out of shape, you can start by walking slowly and going shorter distances. It's cheap. I would say free, but a good pair of walking or cross-training shoes is important. You can do it year round or almost year round, depending on where you live, and you can do it on vacation or when you travel for work or even in a mall. (Two laps around each level of the Mall of America in Minnesota is an hour of walking.)

Walking is much less of a strain on your joints than running, especially if you're very overweight. Also, the great news is that an hour of walking has the same health benefits as a half hour of running. Just make sure you are walking fast enough, as if you are late for an appointment...not strolling. You will be amazed at the difference in weight loss and muscle building when you bump up your pace.

I guarantee if you give yourself two weeks, you will be addicted to the peace of mind, creative free thinking, and sense of overall well being that comes with walking. Problems and concerns really do miraculously dissipate when you walk.

If you want to include friends or family, it's pretty easy to get someone to go on a walk with you, which is great, but don't overlook walking as a perfect opportunity to spend some time with yourself. If others do come with you, don't let them slow you down. If you are a walker and you take a walk with someone who isn't used to fitness walking, you'll be amazed at how strenuous he or she will find it. Here are a few tips to get you started with walking:

Begin with a plan in place. This plan could be a specific distance (around the block) or a block of time (10 minutes), but give yourself an objective to reach. This will help you focus and keep you from just giving up and taking the shortest route home. It also builds success into the activity.

Try walking every day. It is as worthy of every day attention as many of the things we are used to doing every day, such as watching the news. It also works to take three shorter walks instead of one long one.

Start out slowly to warm up your muscles. Then gradually focus on speeding up. The optimum pace is being able to speak (so you know oxygen is getting to your muscles) but not being able to carry on long, extended conversations (so you know you're working hard enough to increase your heart rate). It helps me to visualize how I would walk if I were late for an important appointment and to think of propelling myself forward, as if on the balls of my feet. Remember, anything you do is beneficial.

Trust me, make walking an integral part of your everyday life, and you will lose weight, become stronger, feel more at peace, be more focused and alert, and you will have a clearer perspective on life. I whole-heartedly believe the Nike commercial that said something like, "If there were more walkers, there would be fewer psychiatrists."

Running. It is a great fat burner and a quick exercise to do. However, it is harder on your joints and cardiovascular system (especially if you're overweight). A combination of running and walking is a good alternative. It's also relatively cheap, but you must invest in a decent pair of shoes to prevent aggravating your joints and back. Running appears to have addictive qualities for those who love it.

Biking. This is a fun activity to do with others and a good workout to boot. It brings us back to our childhood and can be incorporated into our daily lives to run errands or visit friends. I have a bike, and when I tour the paths that my city offers, I get a workout and a tour of the city. Biking is a workout, but it doesn't feel like a workout.

Indoor Exercise Bikes. I've used my sister's bike at various times in my life, and I think indoor bikes provide a convenient alternative to outdoor exercises, even though I miss the outdoors when I use one. They are a good workout, but you need to make sure you are keeping up at a pace that will sufficiently raise your heart (make you slightly out of breath). The new ones have great mechanisms for tracking heart rate, calories burned, and the time and distance of your ride.

In-line skating. I sang the praises earlier, but I'll say it again. This is a darned good workout that does wonders for your legs and butt. Wear all the safety equipment, and if you do fall (you're a lot less likely to than you'd think), lean towards your hip and think of rolling. Everything I read about the sport said to invest in expensive skates (over $150) because you'll glide quicker and easier. I started out with the cheap ones, and they do drag, but that's not really a problem when you start out. Going slower is a great comfort.

Swimming. I find swimming to be the most challenging of exercises, but I know people who wouldn't be without it in their lives. If you swim, I think it feeds your soul in a special way, completing an innate connection to the water. It's a great aerobic activity that also tones and strengthens. Lakes are free, and pools are readily found at clubs or community centers.

*   *   *

Active participation in your daily life

My dad weighed 180 pounds and was lean, strong, and muscular with a healthy appetite. He was a farmer for a living and had been since he was 14. He never worked out a day in his life. His occupation kept him slim. Now, few of us have those types of jobs these days. We are pioneers of the cubicles and spend little time on our feet, much less moving. This seems to put us in a mindset that we can never move, that inertia is our way of life, our destiny.

For the longest time I rolled my eyes at the magazine articles that said to incorporate fitness into your life in small ways: parking as far away from stores as possible, taking stairs instead of elevators, and buying a manual rather than gas lawn mower. Well, guess what. These things do work in small steady ways. Most importantly, these little notions set in motion a new way of looking at ourselves as active, moving individuals. In addition to the structured exercise you are going to incorporate into your life, look for ways to take the active path in life. Some ideas are:

Playing with your kids, nieces, nephews or cousins. This is a great work out, and so few adults take the time to play with kids. You will be the most popular dad, mom, aunt, uncle or cousin on the block. Kids love to run, so never underestimate the cardiovascular as well as strength-building benefits of play. If you doubt me, talk to me after an hour with the munchkins.

Cleaning. It has to be done. It's good for your psyche. It involves lots of lifting, bending, walking, and turning, and it keeps you busy and out of the kitchen. Plus, you will be the envy of everyone who sets foot in your house.

Walking on your lunch hour to cleanse your mind. Walk outside if weather permits or maybe at a nearby mall. You don't have to go so fast that you get sweaty. It's more of a mental break and a nice addition to your overall exercise plan.

Walking to shops, restaurants, coffeehouses, and bars in your own neighborhood. Almost everyone lives within walking distance of a business district, yet we are car-happy. Be European, support your local businesses, and get in some more activity.

Redecorating and remuddling (remodeling) projects. There is painting, refinishing woodwork, installing carpet, sewing slipcovers, putting in walls, knocking out walls, replacing bathroom fixtures…and the list goes on. These are all physical activities that will keep you focused and away from food. Many home improvement projects are easy when you break them down into parts and you have the right tools. There are books, CDs, and websites giving explicit help. You will have the house or apartment of your dreams on a budget.

Gardening. Please see the section later in this book on gardening and losing weight. I can't endorse it enough as a great weight loss tool. Yard work (mowing, trimming, watering) is great too.

Get a dog. They're a built-in exercise machine.

The idea here is that you are changing the way you move through life. Choosing activity in small, frequent ways throughout your day and life will make a big difference in your weight loss, and it will give you confidence in your body and the way it moves. You are saying yes to living in small, yet active ways.

         *   *   *

Again, spend some time visualizing your ideal body to help you plan your exercise program. For much of my adult life, my exercise time had always been spent on aerobic exercise with the idea of losing weight, melting fat, and getting smaller. When I went back and spent time visualizing the body I wanted and felt was my authentic body, I realized that it was indeed slimmer, but it was also strong. It occurred to me that my visualizing was shifting from images of slimness to images of strength and firmness. I was also doing some gardening, professionally on the side, and I had noticed how weak I felt, especially when it came to lifting.

In our society, there is awe over the big shoulders, strong arms, and lean waist of a man. It represents strength, certainly, but also self-control, leadership, and virility. To be quite honest, I wanted in on all of that.

Now, it's important to make certain our reasons for wanting something like big arms and shoulders aren't coming from a sense of lacking, that the physique will make up for feelings of inadequacy and diminished self-worth. But I also think that it is completely justifiable and normal to want something that will make us feel and look healthier. Strength training is also great for your body. Increased muscle mass raises your metabolism so you burn fat quicker and easier. It strengthens your joints and increases bone density, which is especially important as you grow older.

*   *.   *

Finding Time Everyday to Exercise

Think of all things you find time for in a day. Many of them need to happen…cooking dinner, driving to work, working, picking up kids from school…but many don't. How about idle TV watching, cruising the Internet or aimless wandering around a mall. I'm confident that you can find an hour out of the day for exercise, especially if you eliminate activities that are doing you no good. Even giving up just one useless activity a day may afford you enough exercise time.

Remember the transformational power of exercise. We make time for what we think is important or for what we can see produces results. Exercise gives us all of those things, but not immediately. Trusting that it is working is crucial at the beginning. Focus on the fact that you are doing one of the most powerful, positive, life-changing activities possible for yourself.

Schedule the time, and let no one waver you. If you keep a schedule, put your exercise hour in it like you would a meeting. Make the 5-6 p.m. hour the exercise hour for you. You do other scheduled activities that you don't look forward to but are necessary. Exercise is one you will like ten minutes into it. Make it as much a part of your day as eating. Would you ever give up dinner? Well, maybe, but you get the drift.

The morning is a great time to exercise. It kick starts your metabolism and gets you burning fat from the beginning of your day. If the idea of rising an hour earlier seems like an impossibility, I can guarantee that the hour of exercise will feel better than the hour of sleep…maybe not at first, but after a week or so.

Get others involved. Your kids want you to be active and healthy, so does your spouse or partner or friends or family members, even if their behavior doesn't show it. Invite joiners along with you. You will be more likely to keep your exercise appointments with yourself if you share the commitment with another. However, on the same note, if you need that time for yourself, don't be afraid to take it. The recharge you gain from the solitary time will benefit everyone in your life in the long run, and they will soon recognize this.

*   *   *

It's kind of boring to concern yourself with how many calories you are burning when you exercise, but it does give you a general idea of what is happening in your body when you work it. You have to burn about 3,500 calories to lose a pound of fat. Consider the following:

Biking, 6 mph (Elvira Gulch in *The Wizard of Oz*)

	240 calories an hour
Biking, 12 mph (pretty darn fast)	410
Jogging, 5 1/2 mph	740
Jogging, 7 mph (pretty good clip)	920
Running, 10 mph (Olympic)	1,280
Swimming, 25 yards a minute	227
Swimming, 50 yards a minute	500
Tennis, singles	400
Walking, 2 mph (an easy stroll)	240
Walking, 3 mph (a peppy stroll)	320
Walking, 4 1/2 mph (as if late)	440

These figures are for someone who is 150 pounds. The more you weigh, the more you burn. Stats are from the American Heart Association and Center for Disease Control.

Chapter 15

Hints for Challenging Times

If you are making positive changes in your life, it may sometimes seem like everyone and everything is out to trip you up. Life is filled with challenges to the overeater who is changing his or her ways, but that is, quite simply, the way life is. People bringing food to the office, holidays at Mom's house, and Old Country Buffet are not going away. **However, what's wonderful and exciting is that you aren't going away either, and you have an enormous capacity for change.** It's this capacity for change that will bring you all the wonderful things you imagine for yourself.

Think of all the little red devils that you encounter along the way as gifts—gifts sent to you by the universe that offer you the opportunity to experience your new way of living. Practice makes prefect, as they say. Each time you don't eat donuts just because they're in the lunchroom and every time you avoid the bowl of chips at a party when you don't really want them, you become better at resisting temptation. I assure you, I know how powerful temptation can be, and you will not resist 100% of the time, but please know that there is a tremendous peace that comes over you when you do not give in to your old ways. When you are confronted with a temptation and do not give in to it, you will literally feel a warmth of positive energy flow through you. Each time you resist, your power grows stronger and stronger. In his book, *Soul Stories,* Gary Zukov refers to temptations as blessings because they in essence warn us of how we will feel if we give in to whatever is tempting us: donuts in the lunchroom, another drink…you know them when they come your way. Consider the following for the inevitable challenges that will confront you.

Free for all lunches at work. If you're tempted by the fact that it's free, think about what it's really costing you. Free cold pizza or congealed chicken almond ding-dong with balls of hard rice is hardly worth delaying the arrival of your true self. If you really do want to eat some of the food, if it really does appeal to you, at least heat it up in a microwave, sit down, eat it slowly, and enjoy it. Stop after one plate and focus on how good it feels to stop eating when you want. Most likely, though, you are better off avoiding it altogether. If you don't have good food with you at work that day, go out and buy yourself something healthy that you really love.

Going out to eat. What inevitably screws me up is the breadbasket. It usually holds very good bread, often with accompanying olive oil and parmesan cheese, and it hits you right as you sit down, when you're most hungry. You may have the constitution to eat one wonderful piece and then sip your wine until the salad comes. If you do, you are my hero. I, however, avoid the bread. My partner has the same relationship with it that I do, so we do not ask for it or ask for it to be taken away.

Unless it's a celebration, like a birthday or some other special day, I always order a salad or the vegetable plate when I go out to eat. Now, there are two things I'd like to point out. First, I love salads and vegetable plates; plus, restaurants are making fabulous versions of both these days. Second, I do not think that if you want to lose weight, salads and vegetable plates are your only options when eating out. Far from it. I just happen to love both, and it makes the whole dining experience simpler and ultimately more enjoyable to not tempt myself too much with something bigger or higher in calories.

The best piece of advice I can offer when eating out is to make no assumptions about what you're ordering. Grilled chicken may be served in a thick, goopy sauce, even if the menu doesn't say so, or your Garden Delight salad may come drowning in dressing. Do yourself the favor of asking. Other helpful restaurant tips to keep in mind:

When your food comes, divide it in half and eat only the first half. Savor the thought of eating it again for lunch tomorrow.

Go the restroom after you order to wash your hands (which you should do anyway). Splash some cold water on your face, take a deep breath, and remind yourself of your new, healthier eating ways.

Order water before you order anything else. It will keep your mouth busy, your thirst quenched (sometimes we mistake hunger for thirst), and it's good for you. It will also fill you up a bit and help keep you from eating more than you would like.

Also, let's not forget that going out to eat is a special affair. I think it's sad that in our society today, going out to eat has become so commonplace that we forget to revel in the joy and excitement. I remember when I was a kid, we would go out to eat once a month at the very most. I would bubble with excitement driving up to the restaurant (and it was usually just a Country Kitchen). I would study the menu and anxiously await my selection. It was all such a big deal. Try bringing that sense of magic back to eating out.

Parties. The free food table is my downfall. I stay as far away as possible. I focus on conversation with people. I make it my goal to walk around the room and chat with everyone that I would regret not getting a chance to chat with. I make light of my relationship with the free food table. "Don't get me started with it; I won't be able to stop!" If there is a rumor of some offering that is not to be missed (someone's homemade guacamole or caramelized onion and brie focacia), I will sneak over to have a small serving and then move away from the table.

I think at the heart of the issue with food at a party is the distance it creates between you and the other people. I've observed overeaters at a party and the way food becomes their focus of attention. How sad when eating becomes more important than catching up with an old friend. An overeater rarely fills up a plate and sits down to enjoy it. He or she partakes in mindless grazing while standing by the table, pretty much in denial that he or she is eating at all. So much less food would be consumed if a plate of favorites was dished up and enjoyed with a drink while sitting down in the living room.

I had always heard, "Never go to a party hungry." I never put much stock in it during my days when I preferred keeping the wall of food between myself and the other guests. But today I believe it to be sound advice because it reinforces staying true to our authentic selves and our authentic eating. Just because we have something put down in front of us does not mean we have to eat it. We are not pigs at a trough. We pick and choose what we eat.

Make your reason to be at the party social rather than gastronomic. Besides keeping you away from the other guests and sabotaging your weight loss goals, it's just plainly and simply rude to eat all the food and leave little for the other guests. Chat with people, and you'll be getting closer to your true self.

If you do eat, have one fabulous, delicious plate, dished up and eaten away from the table. It will be very satisfying if you focus on it and allow it to satisfy you.

Tell yourself that if you don't eat, you can indulge in a couple glasses of wine or a Margarita or two. Although far from low-calorie, drinks are much better than grazing at the food table and don't have the sodium found in snack foods that will puff you up for a couple of days. Also, indulging in them can feel very satisfying. Just keep it to a couple drinks and watch it if you're driving.

Happy Hours. If my pooh-poohing of happy hours still hasn't swayed you enough to avoid them and the idea of drinking around co-workers and perhaps saying or doing something stupid doesn't keep you away, then at least follow these guidelines:

One hour, one drink. Don't waste your whole evening in a dark, smelly bar. The next time you're having a great evening at home, gardening, cooking, watching a great movie, walking or running, stop and think how it would have never happened if you would have overstayed your welcome at happy hour.

Make your drink something you love and will savor. Avoid the two-for-one bar pours or watery tap light beers. Savor a Kahlua and creme, champagne or Tanqueray and tonic. If you are going to do it, do it right. You'll also enjoy your reputation as a person of taste rather than a cheap beer guzzler.

If you have any say over it, **convince the gang to go somewhere without a free food bar.** If there is free food, remember that it's nothing you choose to put into your body. Keep your sights on the fabulous dinner you will have when you get home and how great you will feel from not eating crap.

Family Feasts. If you grew up in a household where food was love (it seems like most overeaters did), family dinners will always be a challenge. In your mind, not eating your mother's cooking is the same as rejecting her love. It's like throwing it back in her face. Take a deep breath and step back a moment.

I realized sometime in my late twenties that I was stuck in a pattern of behavior from which my mother had gotten herself unstuck. I was still compelled to eat everything in sight when I was at her house, but she had allowed herself to break free from food. I observed her eating. It was not crazed and mindless like I somehow felt I had to eat when I was at her house. Sure, she had a lot of food available and always made sure that I knew it, but I realized the pressure to eat was in my head and not coming from her mouth. It was time to break free.

Actually, the mindset that I had remained in was very self-centered. Instead of reaching out to her, I was soaking up all the attention and energy when I was around her by eating everything in sight. It was time to go back and get that 12-year-old little fat boy who stuffed himself full instead of saying how he felt and asking for what he needed. It was time to bring him along with me. Spending time with my mother was all I needed to do to let her know how much I loved her. I'll say it again. Just being there was and is enough. If you aren't able to be with your mother, a letter or phone call will do the same good. My mother takes pride in her cooking and it is praiseworthy, but telling her so is also a way of letting her know how much I love her food. I don't need to eat it all for her to get the gist. Is limitless eating really a compliment to someone? Isn't honest, spoken expression of how delighted you are with someone's cooking so much more true?

Are you holding on to old ideas about eating around your family, ideas that need to be put to rest? Do you still stuff yourself around your family just because that is the way it's been for 10, 20, 30 or more years? Does eating out of control still bring some temporary comfort when you're at your mother's house? Remind yourself that the comfort you receive is false and very fleeting and will betray you quickly. Every time I go to the bathroom at my mom's house I remind myself of this. I think of bathroom breaks as attitude breaks as well.

If eating at your relative's house causes you stress, keep in mind the following. Verbally expressing how you feel about the food frees you from overeating. The cook will get the idea that you love his or her cooking.

Your family will probably find comfort in phrases like "I feel so much better if I eat only half as much" or "I don't get chest pains since I've lost some weight. I better not have seconds." Overeaters are silent about their battles. *No one may have an idea how near to your heart overcoming your overeating is.* Hearing that you are dealing with your food issues may be the greatest news they've heard all month. Our secrets keep us sick.

If it feels good to eat your mom's food (and that is perfectly fine), take some home with you rather than filling up on the spot. I actually bring plastic containers when I go to my mom's house for dinner.

*   *   *

Those Who Challenge Us

Now, it may not be that easy. *The sad truth is that there are people (friends, family, and co-workers) who will try to sabotage our efforts to lose weight.* What they are really doing is trying to prevent losing someone with whom they've gotten very comfortable and familiar. An old friend, if you will. As fat people, we are very susceptible to these saboteurs for a couple of reasons.

If you grew up fat, you are quite likely still in the mindset of trying to fit in and getting people to like you as you are. This sets you up to put other people's needs before your own and, most dangerous, to value other's judgments of you more than you value your own.

Growing up fat also teaches you to be highly sensitive to the feelings of others. Fat people know how disappointment, rejection, and hurt feel and will often go to extremes to help others avoid these feelings.

Growing up with the negative stereotype of fat people being self-centered and indulgent makes you resistant to engage in any sort of behavior that may be viewed as such. Taking care of yourself is anything but these two things. Actually, quite the opposite is true. Only if you care for yourself do you make yourself self-sufficient enough to help others. Facing your insecurities head on rather than eating them away is quite self-less, but this takes time and courage to learn.

These three things make us vulnerable to others when attempting to affect positive change in our lives. Without meaning any harm, those around us have become dependent on our tending to their needs first in the same way that we've become dependent on tending to them. *Also, when you face issues in your life and make steps towards changing, you hold a mirror up to those around you, and they may have to face issues in their lives that they may not be ready to face.* Their behavior is all about themselves and not you. Remember Don Miguel Ruiz's book and the agreement to not take anything personally.

It's tempting to abandon our weight loss plans at this point. It just seems easiest not to rock the boat of our relationships. Plus, the lack of support seems to have a hidden voice saying something to the effect, "So this is your latest tangent. How long is this one going to last? Give it up and let's go get a Dairy Queen!" *Our saboteurs hold so much power because they represent that dark, doubting side of ourselves that would find it so much easier to just stay the way that we are.* Oddly enough, these friends and relatives are actually valuable teachers in our new way of life. They represent how damaging it is to doubt yourself and your dreams of becoming your true self. When you deal with them, you are also taking on the side of yourself that expects you to fail. I've discovered a few essential approaches to these people:

Take the high road. The uncovering of the true you frightens those around you. Be sympathetic and rebound with kindness, and they will see that the new you is not to be feared, but embraced.

Bare your soul. True intentions dissolve the mystery that instills fear. Let those around you know in the simplest terms what is going on inside you. For example, "I'm eating healthy and exercising so I can see my grandchildren grow up," or "I'm sick of being embarrassed of my big belly, and it's hurting my back!"

Invite them along. Part of the sabotage of others comes from a response to feeling left out. To those who have never confronted personal change, it's a terrifying journey. Cook them a fabulous, healthy dinner and bring them on a walk. Warning: you may need to be very persistent.

If all else fails, confront. You are bringing honesty back into your life, so if someone is getting in the way of you achieving your goals, be honest with them. Use "I" when you speak to them. "I feel like abandoning my plan to get healthy because I don't feel supported by you."

*   *   *

And what to do when you just want to eat and eat and eat…

Maybe you should eat something. Incorporate into your psyche that eating a snack, a mini-meal or a regular meal is a good thing and something you have the right to do. Regular eating will not make you gain weight. On the other hand, denying yourself food will almost always send you into a binge.

If you aren't really hungry, try some deep breathing. Belly breathing somehow short-circuits the urge to eat when we aren't really hungry. Take five deep belly breaths (slowly in through your nose, so that your stomach and not your chest expands, and out through your mouth).

When you have the urge to eat past the point of satisfaction, remind yourself that you can eat again in a few hours or tomorrow morning. This is where the whole dieting and denial mindset gets in the way of weight loss. If we think something that we love is bad and we are sneaking a little and can never have it again, we will feel denied, lose control, and binge. Remember, nothing is off limits.

Take a moment to revisualize your true self. Reminding yourself of your ultimate goal will take the thrill off the fleeting moment of eating and place it on the long-term you.

Stop whatever you are doing and take a break. If you want to eat and are not hungry, you probably need a break. When uncomfortable feelings arise, as overeaters we are conditioned to reach for food to squelch the feelings and give us something certain to feel bad about. Instead of reaching for food, step back and take a break. Some deep breaths, a short walk or just some simple zoning out will give you a new perspective.

*   *   *

Daily Renewal

Any change of habit takes, at the very least, two weeks to cement in your psyche. Changing your way of looking at food and eating, I believe, takes much longer. And it requires daily renewal, because you are faced with food every day. However you choose to do this for yourself, **you simply must find a way to refresh the commitment every day.** It could be a morning or evening journal. It could be a calendar with notes and happy faces. Maybe your daily exercise time is your daily renewal when you also meditate on your new attitudes toward food. Maybe you pick up an inspirational book or a book of affirmations and have a daily 15-minute communal with yourself. I give you the homework of creating your daily renewal. This will perhaps become the most important step to finding and supporting your true self.

*   *   *

A Journal

If you've never kept a journal, now is the time to begin. Journals can be anything and everything you want them to be. There are no rules. You don't have to be an A+ speller or a master of grammar. You never have to complete a sentence, and your participles can freely dangle. You can bitch and whine and scream your head off in a journal. ***Keeping a journal is a healthy, freeing, expressive daily, weekly or even monthly ritual that will help immensely in your weight loss process.***

Besides providing a source of daily renewal, writing in a journal organizes and calms racing thoughts. When you feel scattered, confused or overwhelmed, putting pen to paper gets everything in your head out on the table so that your heart can choose what matters the most. List your problems or what is bothering you. Decide on paper which ones you have the ability to change. Write down an action for each positive change. Do not censor yourself when writing in your journal. You do have the God-given ability to effectively handle your problems. Writing in your journal connects you to your heart and your rock-solid gut instinct.

I've kept journals, with greater and lesser frequency, since I was in elementary school. Journaling has been one of my top five greatest tools for losing my weight. When I felt completely alone, writing in my journal gave me someone to talk to. When I gorged on food and hated myself for it, writing in my journal helped me see why I turned to food and helped me remember that I was still a good person and that I should get back on track with healthy eating. When I was first figuring out why I wasn't losing weight, tracking my eating was done in my journal. *To this day, when I need to reconnect to who I really am, I spill out my guts on the page, and everything I truly believe becomes very clear. Priorities in life rise to the top.* A large portion of this book springs from my years of journal entries.

*   *   *

Touchstone

A small memento that you keep on your person, like a ring, bracelet or necklace, can remind you of your new ways of healthy living. What may seem superficial can actually run quite deep. You are not just looking at your grandfather's wedding ring to remind you of how you wish to live a long, happy, and healthy life. You are connecting to your true purposes in life. Touchstones remind you of this until these truths become second nature. Consider adding a touchstone to your life. As mentioned, rings, bracelets, necklaces, and even temporary tattoos or figurines on our desks all work well.

Chapter 16

You Will Never See a Sad Gardener

In addition to quickly becoming the most popular pastime in America, gardening is the perfect activity for the person who wants to lose weight and keep it off. It gives you a soul-enriching activity to lose yourself in, it allows you to grow healthy vegetables and herbs for your new way of eating, and it actually provides very good exercise. I encourage you to consider its possibilities in your life.

You will never see a sad gardener. There is something about working your own little corner of the world. The creativity and pride that comes from it will get you hooked, not to mention the money that you save from growing your own fresh produce. Tomatoes, zucchini, eggplant, green beans, lettuces, and herbs such as basil, cilantro, chives, rosemary, and thyme are just a smattering of what you can grow for yourself.

In our fast-paced, techno-filled world, the need for activities that ground us and slow us down is essential. Gardening grounds your soul and magically brings peace into your life. Gardening works its way into your blood, and it may sound dramatic, but it makes you happy to be alive. You will grow to look very forward to the time you spend in the garden.

A Pot of One's Own

It's wonderful if you have yard space to grow a vegetable garden, but you don't need it. Apartment and townhouse dwellers, renters and homeowners who don't want to dig the earth can grow great vegetables and herbs in pots on the patio, fire escape, windowsill or window box. Container gardening is such a popular trend in gardening because it not only opens up the world of gardening to people without access to a plot of land, but also to people who just want to try their hand at gardening before taking the big plunge. It's also great for those who have physical limitations that keep them from gardening on a larger scale.

Windowsill pots. This is a great way to grow your own herbs in the house year round. Pick your sunniest window, six hours of sun is best, but four will do. Have a separate pot for each herb or combine several in one pot.

Window boxes. These provide another great way to grow your own herbs. Mix in flowers such as nasturtium and pansies (both are edible and look great in salads) or marigolds, petunias or snapdragons for cutting and use as fresh flowers in the house.

Container pots. If you are going to grow more than herbs or flowers, you need to begin with at least a 12-inch pot. Plastic or terra cotta will do, but terra cotta dries out quickly and will need to be watered frequently (everyday). Containers can be strikingly grouped on fire escapes, porches or patios.

*   *   *

Creating a Vegetable Plot in Your Yard

If you don't already have a vegetable garden in your yard, it's easy to create one. You should look for at least a six-by-eight-foot plot to have ample space for the vegetables. Monitor prospective sites for six to eight hours of sun. Four will do in a pinch. Well-drained soil is important. Don't place your plot in a ravine or at a bottom of a hill that won't drain. If you do have a hill to work on, the south side warms up early in the spring and allows for a bit earlier planting. Also, the tendency for most is to stick the vegetable garden back behind the garage. If that's your only option, it's fine, but it actually works much better to put the vegetable garden as near to the house as possible. Easy accessibility encourages the gardener to use the garden. Plus, there is nothing more attractive than a well-tended veggie plot.

*   *   *

Prepping Your Newly Found Garden

Killing grass. If you have the time (about 6 weeks), laying six to ten layers of newspaper (inks are soy based these days) over the area of your new garden and anchoring them with stones or bricks will kill the grass.

Using a flat-bottomed spade to remove sod is a little more labor-intensive, but doable if your plot isn't too big. Using a sweeping motion, lift the spade into the air and swing it down to skim the turf grass off the surface of the soil. Don't dig and turn the grass into the garden. The rhizomes will merely resprout and send the shoots the way of the sun. Put the removed sod in your compost bin (more on this later).

Prepping soil. Especially if you have a newer home, your soil may be clay-like. You can improve clay soil by working in leaves, grass clippings or sawdust into the clay. Improving your soil will be an ongoing endeavor. You can also have a small load of black dirt brought in and rototill (available at rental centers) it into the clay.

Whether you have clay soil, sandy soil (not bad for vegetables) or decent black soil, you will need to either double-dig or rototill your new garden space. Double digging is just as it says. With a spade or shovel, dig down one foot and turn over the soil. Then do it once again.

It never hurts to have your soil tested for the amount of organic matter and acidity. You can get a kit to send in a sample from your county extension agency. Nearly all vegetable plots need continuous soil improvements. Composted manure (available at nurseries and garden centers), leaves, grass clippings or your own compost should be added when you create your garden and every year thereafter.

If your vegetable garden borders grass, you will want to install edging (available in garden and home improvement centers) to prevent the grass from creeping into your sacred place. You can also create an edging with old bricks, rocks or chunks of concrete.

*   *   *

Vegetables for Containers and Your Garden

Your likes and favorite recipes will determine the vegetables you choose to tend in your garden. Consider these common ones that will provide you with a plethora of opportunities for cooking.

Cucumbers. Choose "bush" cucumbers for containers or small gardens. There are two basic varieties (slicing and pickling), and both have "bush" sub-varieties. And the pickling varieties work great in salads and on sandwiches. Keep your cucumbers and zucchini as far apart as possible to prevent cross-pollinating between the two.

Eggplant. Wonderful for containers or the garden because the flowers are beautiful (they look like orchids) and the plants themselves are really quite small. Eggplants respond well to extra fertilizer (work some extra organic matter such as leaves around their base). Grill them for a real treat or make Baba Ganouj (see recipe section).

Green beans. Look for the "bush" variety for the container or small space garden. An eight-foot long row will produce a decent amount of beans for the summer.

Hot peppers. These are beautiful and a great punch in your cooking. Use them for salsa, spicing up marinades, and adding a little extra zing in just about anything.

Lettuces. These are delightful vegetables to have in the container or regular garden. Get yourself a salad-spinner to help in washing the dirty greens. If you don't have a spinner, once you've washed the greens, roll them in paper towels to dry. Remember, as they are growing, the younger the leaf, the sweeter and tenderer it will be. Varieties include simpson, bon vivant blend, red sails, buttercrunch head lettuce, and mesclun mix (a blend of greens and herbs).

Spinach. It's easy to grow and so healthy, and it's great as the base for a salad or to cook with (omelets, pizzas, and great side dishes).

Tomatoes. Grow these easily in containers or two feet apart in your garden. You will either need to tie the plants to stakes or grow them inside tomato cages for support (tomatoes are vines). Clip off the leaves on the lower third of the plants to send extra energy to the fruits. You can grow many varieties including cherry (excellent for salads), roma (excellent for making oven-dried tomatoes), beefsteak, big boy, early girl and brandywine. Because of the amount of time needed to produce fruits, it's best to start with started plants available at nurseries and garden centers.

Zucchini. These can be grown in containers as well as in the garden plot. A versatile vegetable with its own distinct flavor, it also picks up the flavor of the foods with which it's cooked. Also known as summer squash, the two basic varieties are green and yellow. Two plants will keep a household very well fed all summer. Use it in stir-fries, stews, to grill, sauté, and in quick bread.

*   *   *

Herbs for Containers and Your Garden

Basil. Sow lots of it to make enough pesto to freeze for winter use (see recipe section). Numerous varieties are available including a purple ruffles, which looks great in salads. An annual, it must be reseeded every year.

Chives. This is a perennial (returns every year) that every home needs. It's one of the most versatile herbs with an onion-like flavor, which is great in meats, vegetables, potato topping, salads, and eggs. Garlic chives can replace garlic in dishes.

Cilantro. Easy to grow, it often reseeds itself for the following year. A staple in Mexican cooking, it's a must for salsa, and you will find hundreds of other uses. It has a fresh, zippy taste. It is also known as coriander.

Lemon Balm. This perennial spreads profusely. The intense fragrance is a nice addition wherever you would like the presence of lemon.

Oregano. A staple in Italian cooking, this perennial pairs wonderfully with tomatoes and all your meat recipes. Look for the Greek strains for a more intense, pungent flavor.

Parsley. Besides being a natural diuretic and breath cleanser, parsley is a flavorful addition to salads and vegetable dishes. You can pick from curly or flat leafed varieties.

Rosemary. An annual in the north and a perennial in the south, I swear its taste has addictive properties. It is excellent with chicken, with vegetables, and in salads. The aroma is so pleasing, it's nice to just have a plant around the house to touch and smell from time to time.

Sage. This pleasing, homey-tasting herb is a nice addition to meats, dressings and sauces. It's an annual, but it will sometimes survive a winter.

Thyme. It goes well with poultry and meatloaves. A perennial, the creeping variety works well in the garden around stones or as a groundcover.

*   *   *

The Best Annual Flowers for Your Garden

The following is a list of simple, beautiful annual flowers for use in mixing with herbs in your containers or for borders and accent plantings in your vegetable garden. Plant this list, and you will also have a great collection of flowers for cutting and bringing into the house for arrangements.

Bells of Ireland. Seen all the time in professional bouquets, the plant's green and bell-like flowers ride up and down a long stem.

Celosia. The plume and cockscomb varieties in their jeweled tones are often seen for sale on the streets of New York for big money. You can grow your own for visual impact in your house.

Dusty Miller. Unusual, soft, gray leaves will add an unexpected color and texture to the garden as well as bouquets.

Larkspur. Tall, grand stems of vibrant colored flowers will be the vertical touch to your garden and indoor arrangements.

Marigold. Planted more for their fall color than indoor appeal, they are also said to repel harmful insects from the garden. They work well as borders.

Nasturtium. Beautiful and edible flowers make these plants wonderful. Soak the seeds overnight before planting or slice the shell of the seed with a knife.

Pansy. This staple of the garden and sweet addition to arrangements can be planted early in the spring, since they are cold-tolerant. Every northern gardener needs some in April to get out of the winter doldrums.

Snapdragons. These two-toned flowers are available in a wide mix of colors.

Zinnia. In my opinion, these are the un-sung heroes of the garden. Available in so many sizes and colors, it's impossible to beat their vibrant colors.

*   *   *

Planting Your Containers

Drainage holes. It is best to use containers with drainage holes; however, if you have an interesting container you would like to use that doesn't have a hole on the bottom, by all means, use the interesting pot. Plants need good drainage to keep their roots from smothering and rotting in standing water. If your container doesn't have drainage built in, add at least an inch of gravel, stones or broken terra cotta-pot shards to the bottom of the pot to keep the roots from living in the excess water. This is also a good technique, if you do have a drainage hole, to help keep the soil from washing through the hole when you water.

Planting medium. Store bought planting mixes are great or you can use soil from your yard or garden mixed with 1/3 peat moss or vermiculite (a natural substance) to lighten the soil and help the roots breathe. It is also helpful to add some organic matter such as leaves or grass clippings to enrich the soil.

Spacing and depth. If you're planting seeds, follow the directions on the packet. Vegetable plants should be centered in the middle of the pot and at basically the depth at which they are growing in the pack. If you are planting multiple herbs in a pot, space them at least two inches apart.

Watering. Container gardens will need to be watered at least every other day and every day in the very hot days of summer, unless it rains. Plants that are allowed to dry out produce small, dry, irregularly-shaped vegetables. Like us, vegetables are nearly all water.

*   *   *

Planting your Garden

Once you have prepared your soil, it is a good idea to plot your garden on paper. Your plants should be at least two feet apart.

Intermingle your vegetable and flower plants for visual effect and to encourage the bees to help pollinate.

After you have planted your garden, it is a good idea to mulch or cover the unplanted areas with leaves, grass clippings, or straw to discourage weeds and to retain moisture. Commit to daily weeding to keep weeds from competing with your plants, and water at least four times a week (unless it rains).

*   *   *

Composting

Composting goes hand in hand with gardening. It reduces the amount of trash you generate in your kitchen, and it creates better gardening soil with which to work. You can recycle you kitchen scraps (no meat or grease), yard waste (unless it's been chemically treated), leaves, and even human hair to create a rich mixture to add to your soil. The concept grosses out some people, but trust me that the difference it makes to your vegetables will make it a worthwhile practice.

You can buy fancy compost bins or build your own out of a wood frame and screen. You can also have a pile or heap going without a container. The bin or pile must be three feet by three feet to get to the temperature needed (140 degrees) to compost. It also must be able to breathe so be sure your container has holes or spaces for circulation.

Composting basics. Any organic material will break down over time, but you can speed the process by mixing brown (carbon) and green (nitrogen) materials together. Brown materials include straw, leaves, and sawdust. Green materials include grass clippings, weeds, and most kitchen waste. Mixing the two and keeping it moist will give you good compost in about eight weeks. Stir your mixture every week, and feel free to add coffee grounds, eggshells, and all other natural kitchen waste to the pile. Break down stalks and thicker materials to speed the composting. Incorporate your summer's composting into your garden in the fall or early spring.

*   *   *

In addition to providing you with joy and baskets of great food, gardening is great exercise. Gardening is now counted toward the Center for Disease Control's recommendation for getting a cumulative 30 minutes or more of moderate exercise every day. Defined by the CDC as weeding, trimming, and raking, gardening burns about 450 calories an hour for men and 350 calories an hour for women. Experts tell us we need to burn about 3,500 extra calories to lose a pound of fat. An hour of gardening a day for a week almost does that by itself.

When people tell me they dislike gardening, I feel they are simply overwhelmed by the prospect. Gardening is not a Herculean undertaking that has to take your entire weekend away from you. Now, the great thing is that it can if you want it to, but it doesn't have to. Gardening can be an extremely expressive, calming, grounding, and fun little hobby or else it can be an entire way of life. For most gardeners, it's somewhere in between.

Find one small project with which to start. Grow a tomato in a container on the patio. Plant a pot full of your favorite herbs to set on your porch. Try an interesting combination of annual flowers in a planter on your front step. Or take the plunge and plant a vegetable garden. Whatever you choose to try, break it into several smaller projects, take your time, and never forget that it is supposed to be fun. You will be glad you did, and your friends will be so impressed.

Chapter 17

Recipes

Your favorite recipes are your biography. They tell a story about you. The more you embrace food as the glorious thing that it is, the more important your favorite recipes will become to you. The following is a collection of my favorite recipes. Some of them may not seem like they belong in a book about weight loss, but, believe me, they do. The more you give yourself what you really want to eat, the less likely you will feel denied and start stuffing yourself with whatever is available.

If you would like to take some of these recipes and make them your favorites as well, please do. The important thing is to incorporate your favorite foods (in moderation) into your everyday eating.

Some of the recipes represent specific periods of my life and how I was relating to food. Most represent the most recent period of my life when I decided to make food a passion, something to be enjoyed and celebrated.

*   *   *

Breakfast Foods

Bran Muffin

I perfected these in my late 20's when I was obsessed with fiber. I tried to make them fat free, but I soon learned that you have to have a little fat in your baked goods if you want them to be at all enjoyable. Experts at baking would concur whole-heartedly. The apple adds extra fiber and moisture.

1 1/4 cup all bran or 100% bran cereal

1 cup flour

2 tsp. baking soda

1 1/4 cup brown sugar

2 tsp. cinnamon

1/2 tsp. salt

1 cup shredded apple

1/2 cup raisins

1/3 cup vegetable oil

1/2 cup milk

2 eggs

1 tbsp. grated or minced orange rind

1/2 cup apple sauce

Preheat oven to 350° and spray a muffin tin with non-stick cooking spray. Combine dry ingredients (bran cereal through salt) in a large bowl. Stir in apple and raisins. Create a well in the dry ingredients. In another large bowl beat the wet ingredients (vegetable oil through apple sauce) with a wire whisk until slightly frothy. Pour wet ingredients into well of dry ingredients and stir until well-incorporated. Fill each muffin cup 2/3 full and bake for 25 minutes or until muffin springs back when touched. Remove muffins from pan immediately and cool. Makes about 16 small muffins.

*   *   *

The Perfect Two-Egg Omelet (Two versions)

An omelet is an art form, but also a skill that can be easily learned. There is plenty of room for your own stamp of creativity with omelets, but you must start out with the right formula. The first is the ultimate high-rising omelet, but a little putzier. The second will do just fine when you have less time.

Two-Egg Omelet (Version One)

2 eggs

1/2 tbsp. olive oil or non-stick spray

1/4 cup sliced or chopped onions

1/4 cup grated cheese (any kind you wish)

1 tbsp. water

Salt and pepper

Spray pan with non-stick cooking spray or heat the olive oil on high for two minutes. Add onions and sauté for three minutes or just until they begin to soften. Move onions to one side of the pan and reduce heat to medium high. In two separate bowls, separate the yolks from the whites of the two eggs and beat separately until frothy. Combine the yolks and whites in one bowl and pour into the pan. Cook until sides begin to harden. Add cheese and water to pan and cover for 3 minutes or until puffed up. Uncover. Carefully slide spatula or turner under one half of omelet and flip over. Slide spatula or turner under omelet and lift or slide onto plate. Salt and pepper to taste.

*   *   *

Two-Egg Omelet (Version Two)

2 eggs

1/2 tbsp. olive oil or non-stick spray

1/4 cup sliced or chopped onions

1/4 cup grated cheese (whichever kind you wish)

1 tbsp. water

Salt and pepper

Spray a non-stick pan with non-stick cooking spray or heat the olive oil on high for two minutes. Add onions and sauté for three minutes or just until they begin to soften. Move onions to one side of the pan and reduce heat to medium high. Break the two eggs into one bowl, beat until frothy and pour into the pan. Cook until sides begin to harden. Add cheese and water to pan and cover for 3 minutes or until puffed up. Uncover. Carefully slide spatula or turner under one half of omelet and flip over. Slide spatula or turner under omelet and lift or slide onto plate. Salt and pepper to taste.

Spinach and Mushroom additions. Sauté mushrooms with the onions and add fresh spinach with the cheese to wilt when you cover omelet.

*   *   *

E-Z Egg Bake for Two

This can be prepped the night before and baked in the morning. It's kind of like an easy, poor man's soufflé.

4 eggs or how ever many you like

Milk (skim is fine)

1/2 cup chopped onions

1/2 cup sliced mushrooms

1/2 cup shredded or crumbled cheese of your choice

1 tbsp. olive oil

Non-stick cooking spray

Salt and pepper

Preheat oven to 350°. Sauté onions, peppers and mushrooms in olive oil for five minutes and set aside. Crack eggs into bowl and for each egg used add a half shell of milk to eggs. If you use more than four eggs, increase the amount of vegetables and cheese. Decrease if you use fewer. Whisk until frothy. Add vegetables and cheese and stir until well combined. Salt and pepper. Pour into sprayed or greased casserole. Bake for 40 minutes or until slightly firm and raised around the edges. Serve immediately.

*   *   *

Oatmeal in an Instant

Microwaved oatmeal in a cookbook? I included it because I think it's such a delicious, quick, and easy breakfast. Plus, it's very inexpensive.

Pour 3/4 cup of instant oats in a microwave-safe dish and add enough water to make it moist and almost soupy. Microwave on high for two to three minutes, depending on your microwave. Add a small dollop of butter, a tablespoon of brown sugar and a 1/4 cup of milk and you're ready to go.

*   *   *

Buttermilk Pancakes

When I was in early elementary school, two meals got me really excited: split-pea soup and pancakes. I looked forward to these like Christmas morning. They were my special treat meals, and to this day they both take me back to being with my mother in our farmhouse kitchen. You have to understand the kind of joy I got from these meals. I had to have been born with a pancake and split pea soup gene. This is the kind of experience a person should have with food. It's fun to revisit recipes now that I can enjoy them in moderation.

1 1/2 cups flour

1/2 tsp. baking soda

3/4 tsp. salt

1 tbsp. sugar

1/4 cup vegetable shortening

1 egg

1 1/2 cup buttermilk

Mix first four dry ingredients in a large bowl. Spoon in the vegetable shortening. Add the egg and buttermilk and beat well. Fry on a lightly greased griddle or skillet until each side is golden brown. Serve with maple syrup or cottage cheese and jam. Makes about 16. There is an endless list of ingredients that you can add to the batter: mashed bananas, walnuts, raisins, dried fruits, chocolate chips, etc.

*   *   *

Appetizers and Snacks

Bruschetta

This is a simple appetizer for a summer meal. It tastes so fresh and feels so light in your belly.

2 medium tomatoes, diced

1 small onion, diced

1/4 cup basil, coarsely chopped

1/3 cup fresh, grated Parmesan cheese

2 garlic cloves, minced

1 tbsp. red pepper flakes

Pinch of salt

Pinch of pepper

Olive oil

1 small baguette, sliced into 16 slices, at a diagonal

Preheat broiler. Combine tomatoes, onion, basil, cheese, garlic, red pepper flakes, salt and pepper in a medium bowl. Arrange baguette slices on a cookie sheet covered with aluminum foil. (Oil the foil with a little olive oil). Drizzle a touch of olive oil on each slice and top with a healthy sized spoonful of the mixture. Place under broiler until lightly browned, about 3-4 minutes. Serve at once.

*   *   *

Roasted Head of Garlic

This is a wonderful, potent appetizer, and it is also a great basis for garlic mashed potatoes. Serve with sliced baguettes or crackers.

Preheat oven to 400°. Slice the top 1/2 inch of the bulb off and discard. Drizzle one tbsp. of olive oil over the bulb and place in a casserole. Fill the casserole with water one third of the way up the garlic bulb and cover. Bake for 45 minutes or until bulb bubbles with a brown caramel. Serve the roasted head on a platter with the baguette slices or crackers and let the diners pop out the cloves with a knife.

*   *   *

Shirley's Veggie Dip

My mom always mixed up some of this to have on hand and eat with carrots when she needed a nibbly. It's a pretty good way to get your green leafies. A little dab goes a long way.

1 cup mayonnaise (can be low fat or fat-free)

1 cup sour cream (can be low fat or fat-free)

1 tsp. salt

2 tbsp. dried onion

2 tsp. dill weed

2 tsp. dried parsley.

1 tbsp. garlic powder

Cream all ingredients together in a small bowl and chill at least three hours before serving. Slice up carrots, cucumbers, radishes, celery, cauliflower, broccoli, cherry tomatoes, green onions, zucchini, sweet peppers, eggplant and whatever else you wish for dipping.

*   *   *

Glorious Guacamole and Homemade Chips

This is a little high in fat (albeit the good kind), but packs a lot of vitamins and satisfaction. The homemade chips help you forego the fat and salt, but feel free to use store bought chips for the ease and simplicity.

2 large, ripe avocados

Juice of 1 lime

2 small tomatoes, chopped finely

1/4 cup cilantro leaves, chopped finely

1/3 cup onion, chopped coarsely

2 hot peppers of your choice, seeded and minced finely

Cut avocados in half, stick a knife in pit and pull out. Scoop out the flesh with a tablespoon, put in a medium bowl and mash to your desired consistency with a fork (a few lumps are tasty to run into). Add remaining ingredients and blend together.

*   *   *

Homemade Tortilla Chips

4 12-inch flour tortillas

Non-stick cooking spray

Preheat oven to 300°. Cut your tortillas like a pie into 8 pieces and arrange on a cookie sheet sprayed with non-stick cooking spray. Bake in the oven for 15 minutes or until crispy. Remove and serve warm or at room temperature. Makes 32 large chips.

*   *   *

Pico de Gallo Salsa

This is a chunkier version of salsa.

1 cup coarsely chopped onion

2 cups coarsely chopped tomato

1 cup chopped green pepper

1/4 cup chopped cilantro

3 garlic cloves, minced

1 jalapeno pepper or other hot pepper, seeded and minced

1 tbsp. sugar

Juice of one lime

1/4 cup dark beer (optional)

Salt and pepper to taste

Combine all ingredients in a medium bowl and allow to set for 30 minutes before serving. Great with homemade chips.

*   *   *

Purple Reigns Eggplant Dip (or Baba Ganouj)

I would grow eggplant even if it didn't produce such a delicious and beautiful fruit. The flowers are so striking and unique that the plant really belongs in the flower bed. Roasting the eggplant halves on the grill gives the dip a special, smoky flavor. This stuff is so good it's addictive. Plus, it's so healthy.

2 eggplants, cut in half, lengthwise

1 tsp. olive oil

6 garlic cloves, finely minced
Juice of half of a lemon
One inch square piece of lemon rind, finely minced
1/3 cup tahini (a sesame seed butter available in natural food sections, ethnic food sections or sometimes by the peanut butter)
Pinch of salt
Preheat oven to 350°. Place a sheet of aluminum foil on a cookie sheet, lightly oil it and place the four eggplants, cut side down on the foil. Bake for 35 minutes. You can also grill the eggplants on an outdoor grill until browned. Allow to cool. Scoop the flesh of the fruits into the bowl of a food processor and add remaining ingredients. Puree until well blended and looking like a malted milk. Garnish with parsley and paprika for color (it's a little bland looking). Serve with sliced cucumbers and wedges of whole-wheat pita bread.

*   *   *

Pesto

Basil should be in every garden. The sweet smell and taste are the outdoor perfume of August and September. This recipe for pesto, and everyone should have a recipe for pesto, uses spinach. Besides using up less basil, it keeps the pesto from turning brown, which it is apt to do. If you prefer, replace the spinach in the recipe with the same amount of basil. Pesto is mildly addictive and is not only great as an appetizer with slices of baguettes or crackers, it is also wonderful tossed with pasta or as a meat marinade. Do yourself a favor and make enough to freeze in small freezer bags to have all year. It's a wonderful bright spot in the long winter.

10 cloves of garlic
1/4 cup packed basil
3/4 cup packed spinach leaves, well washed and dried
1 small tomato, quartered

1/3 cup walnuts, toasted for 2 minutes under the broiler or sun-flower seeds

1/3 cup shredded or grated Parmesan

In a food processor, with the chopping blade, chop the garlic. Add basil, spinach, and tomato and process. Add walnuts (or sunflower seeds) and Parmesan and chop until well processed. Add a tbsp. of olive oil if pesto is a bit dry. Serve on sliced baguettes, crackers or toss with pasta.

*   *   *

Pesto Brie Bites

Preheat broiler. Cut a small baguette into 12 slices. Lightly oil each slice and top with a tbsp. of pesto. Top with a piece of Brie the diameter of a nickel and place under broiler until brie is melted and bubbling, about 2-3 minutes. Serve at once.

*   *   *

Salads

Green Bean, Sun-dried Tomato and Walnut Salad

2 cups green beans, trimmed and cut in half

1 cup oven-dried tomatoes (see below), chopped into one inch square pieces

1/2 cup walnuts, coarsely chopped

1/4 cup balsamic vinegar

2 tbsp. olive oil

3 cloves garlic, finely minced

Pinch of salt

Pinch of pepper

Steam green beans until slightly tender, but still crisp and bright green, about five minutes. Strain and cool. In a large bowl, combine green beans and tomatoes. Roast walnuts under broiler for about two minutes, or until brown and crackly, and allow to cool. In a small bowl, whisk together vinegar, olive oil, garlic, salt and pepper. Pour dressing over beans and tomatoes and top with walnuts. Toss salad and allow to set for at least an hour before serving.

*   *   *

Oven-dried Tomatoes or Roasted Romas

Preheat oven to 200°. Cut as many Roma tomatoes as you wish in half lengthwise. Arrange about 1/2 inch apart, cut side down on a cookie sheet with lightly oiled aluminum foil on it. With the oven door propped slightly open, bake for approximately eight hours or until wrinkly and dry. Remove from cookie sheet and store in an airtight container for up to a month.

*   *   *

Mother's Layered Salad

This is always a treat when Mom makes it, not only because it's delicious, but it also gives me something healthy to munch on at the family dinner table.

1 head of iceberg lettuce, chopped into bite size pieces

1/2 cup celery, chopped

1/2 cup onion, chopped

1/2 cup mushrooms, sliced

Half of a 10 oz. pkg. frozen peas, thawed

3/4 cup cheddar cheese, shredded (can be low fat or fat-free)

3/4 cup Swiss cheese, shredded (can be low fat or fat-free)

2 tbsp. sugar

1 cup sour cream (can be low fat or fat-free)

1 cup mayonnaise (can be low fat or fat-free)

10 bacon strips (can be turkey or soy), cooked, drained and crumbled

In a 9 1/2 by 11 inch cake pan, layer the ingredients from the bottom
up in the following order: lettuce, celery, onions, mushrooms, peas
and cheeses. Whisk together sour cream, mayonnaise, sugar and salt
and pepper in a small bowl and spread over salad. Sprinkle bacon on
top of dressing. Cover tightly and refrigerate overnight to marinate.

*   *   *

Sweet Breath and Good Taste: Minnesota Tabouli

Parsley controls bad breath, takes excess water from your body,
strikingly garnishes anything it comes close to and adds a clean, fresh,
distinctive taste to just about anything.

Officially Middle Eastern in origin, my variation is clearly a
Minnesota Tabouli. I don't care for the taste of mint in Tabouli, so I
leave it out, but you can add about 2 tbsp., if you like. I also tend to
keep adding whatever is ripe in the garden to the salad. It's a light
salad and very fresh and healthy tasting. Serve it with pita bread or as
a side dish to just about anything.

1 cup dry bulgur wheat

1 cup boiling water with a few slices of lemon in it

2 tbsp. olive oil

3 cloves garlic, minced

2 large green onions, thinly sliced

Shake of pepper

1 cup of finely minced parsley

1 large diced tomato

1/2 cup garbanzo beans

1 small diced cucumber

Combine wheat, water and lemon slices in a bowl, cover and let sit for 20 minutes while the wheat absorbs the water. Remove lemon slices, mince and return to wheat. Add olive oil, garlic and green onions and stir together. Cover and let set for one hour. Add remaining ingredients, stir and serve. Makes about six servings.

*   *   *

Simple Tomato and Red Onion Salad

This salad is so delicious and tastes very much like the fabulous Tomato Salad at Buca's Restaurant in Minneapolis. Serve it with really good bread to help soak up the wonderful sauce.

4 large tomatoes (any variety, but Roma), cored and sliced into 1/2 inch wedges

1 small red onion, sliced into 1/4 inch slices

1/3 cup white wine vinegar (can substitute other vinegars)

3 tbsp. olive oil

6 cloves garlic, finely minced

1/4 cup minced basil

Pinch of salt

Pinch of pepper

1 tbsp. sugar

Arrange tomato wedges and onion slices, alternately, on a plate or platter. Whisk together vinegar, oil, garlic, basil, salt, pepper, and sugar in a small bowl. Pour dressing over tomatoes and onions. Allow to marinate for one hour before serving. You can also top with 1/2 cup feta cheese and 1/2 cup sliced kalamata olives.

*   *   *

Spinach Salad (serves two)

Spinach gives you it all: fiber, vitamins, and great color! This salad is a staple in my eating.

4 cups loosely packed, washed spinach, coarsely chopped

1/2 cup red onion, thinly sliced

1/2 apple, thinly sliced

1/4 cup almonds

1/3 cup crumbled feta or goat cheese

Arrange spinach on two dinner plates with onion and apple scattered on top. Sprinkle walnuts and feta cheese over salads. Drizzle the desired amount of the following dressing on the salad:

Garlic Vinaigrette

1/4 cup olive oil

1/2 cup balsamic vinegar

6 garlic cloves, finely minced

1/4 cup parsley, finely chopped

1 tbsp. sugar or honey

Combine ingredients in a covered jar and shake for approximately 30 seconds. Allow to set for 30 minutes before serving.

*   *   *

Tahini Chop-Chop Dressing

This will make you a dedicated green leafie eater. It is great as a salad dressing or fresh veggie dip. Please give it a try.

4 tbsp. fresh squeezed lemon juice

1 cup sesame tahini (sesame seed butter found in natural food section, ethnic food section or sometimes by the peanut butter)

2 cups water (or until you achieve the thickness you like)

1/4 cup fresh cilantro, finely chopped

Salt and pepper to taste

2 garlic cloves, finely minced

Place lemon juice, tahini, cilantro and garlic in food processor or blender. Process until mixed and slowly add water until you reach the desired thickness (like a thin malted milk). Transfer to small container, add salt and pepper to taste and cover. Refrigerate. It will keep for about two weeks, just add water as needed to thin.

*   *   *

Peanut Dressing

Addictive. Great on salads, pasta, and chicken. Not the lowest in fat, but you don't need much. The flavor is very intense.

3/4 cup peanut butter, creamy or chunky or low-fat or Peanut Wonder (low-fat peanut butter, found in the natural food section)

2 cups low-sodium chicken bouillon broth

1/3 cup fresh lime juice

2 tbsp. honey

1 tbsp. soy sauce, reduced sodium preferably

3 tbsp. fresh ginger, peeled and minced finely

1 tsp. dried and crushed red pepper

Mix peanut butter and chicken broth together in a medium saucepan. Add remaining ingredients and heat over medium heat, stirring constantly until sauce is thickened, about five minutes. Can be served warm or cool. Re-warm over medium heat, adding water if necessary.

*   *   *

Cucumber Tastes Like Summer Salad

Nothing tastes more like summer than cucumber, except for maybe sweet corn and tomatoes. This salad is a wonderful side dish anytime and can be used as a dressing on greens. Also great on a baked potato.

4 cucumbers, sliced into 1/4 inch thick coins

1 small onion, peeled and sliced into thin rings

1/2 cup cider vinegar

1/4 cup sugar

1/2 tsp. celery seed

1/2 tsp. dill weed

2 tbsp. salt

Salt and pepper to taste

1 small red pepper, sliced thinly

Mix cucumbers with onion and 2 tbsp. salt in a medium bowl. Place a small plate on cucumbers and onion and allow to set for two hours. Drain accumulated liquid off. Mix or shake vinegar, sugar, celery seed, dill weed, salt and pepper in a bowl or covered jar until mixed. Pour over cucumbers. Add red pepper and stir. Allow to marinate for an hour at room temperature before serving. Serves four.

*   *   *

Soups

Fresh Tomato Soup

This is my mom's recipe. She is the greatest cook I know, partly because she keeps her dishes simple, knowing what goes with what to create a subtle, delicious impact. This soup is so easy, you could make it every night.

5 tomatoes, diced into 1 inch cubes

1/2 cup chopped onion

1 tablespoon sugar

2 cups milk (skim or 1%)

1 tsp. baking soda

Pinch of salt and pepper

Bring tomatoes, onion and sugar to boil in a large pan and reduce to simmer for 10 minutes. Heat milk (not to boiling) in a separate pan and add to tomatoes. Gently stir. Add soda and watch it foam! Gently stir, again. Add salt and pepper to taste. Serve with a salad, crusty bread and crisp white wine, if you're so inclined. Makes two great big bowls, but plan on making a second pot when you're done with the first.

*   *   *

Split Pea Soup with Ham

This is my other favorite childhood food. I love making it on a crisp fall day.

1 ham bone or 2 cups cubed turkey ham

10 cups cold water

1 lb. green split peas

1 large onion, diced

2 large carrots, sliced into coins

2 large parsnips, julienned into thick, matchstick sized pieces

Salt and pepper.

In a large stockpot filled 3/4 full of water, place ham bone and peas and bring to boil. Reduce to medium high and gently boil two hours. Remove ham bone and add carrots and parsnips. Reduce heat to medium and simmer for half of an hour or until soup is creamy. Add salt and pepper to taste. Serve with a salad and crispy bread.

*   *   *

Green Leafies and Side Dishes

Broiled Green Beans

These taste like a cross between green beans and French fries.

    1 lb. fresh green beans, trimmed

    1 tbsp. olive oil

    Salt and pepper

Toss trimmed green beans in a bowl with oil and spread one layer thick on a cookie sheet. Place under broiler for 7 minutes, take out and stir and put under broiler for another 5 minutes or until crispy and you can smell the beans. Season with salt and pepper to taste.

         *   *   *

Garlic Mashed Potatoes

Highly flavorful and very comforting. Pair with roast chicken and tomato salad for a wonderful taste sensation.

    6 white potatoes

    2 chicken bouillon cubes

    Water

    1/2 cup onion, chopped fine

    1 head roasted garlic, cloves squeezed out (see earlier recipe)

    A quick splash of skim milk

    1 tbsp. fat free sour cream

    Salt and pepper to taste

Scrub and cut up potatoes into one-inch pieces. You may peel the potatoes if you so desire. Put in a large saucepan with bouillon and just enough water to cover. Bring to boil and cook until you can pierce a potato with a fork and it slides off. Drain liquid. Add onion, garlic cloves, milk and sour cream to potatoes and beat with an electric mixer, potato masher or wire whisk until smooth and creamy. Season with salt and pepper to taste. Serves four.

*   *   *

Lutheran Rice & Beans

The rice and beans complement each other and provide a meal's worth of vegetarian protein in one dish. No matter how hard I try to make a Bohemian or ethnic entree, it always seems to have a decidedly Minnesotan bent…thus the name.

1 medium onion, coarsely chopped

5 garlic cloves, minced

1 jalapeno chili pepper, minced

2 tbsp. olive oil

1 cup uncooked brown rice

2 cups water

1 14 1/2 oz. can diced tomatoes

Salt and pepper to taste

1 can kidney beans with juice

1 small can of corn, drained

Heat olive oil in a large skillet pan or Dutch oven on medium high heat. Sauté onions, garlic and jalapeno for a about 3 minutes. Reduce heat to low and add rice. Continue to sauté until rice is browned. Add water, tomatoes, salt and pepper and cook until rice is done, about 50 minutes. Add beans with juice and drained can of corn and cook on medium high for five minutes. Serves four.

*   *   *

Main Events

Grilled Vegetable Sandwich

This sandwich is designed for the grill, but you can try grilling veggies under the broiler or on top of the stove in a ribbed frying pan.

1/3 cup olive oil

4 tbsp. balsamic vinegar

6 garlic cloves, minced

1/4 cup chopped parsley

Dijon mustard

Salt and pepper to taste

Round loaf of whole grain, sourdough or your favorite bread, sliced in half

1 small eggplant, cut crosswise into 1/2 inch slices

2 medium zucchini, cut lengthwise into 1/2 inch slices

4 large Portobello mushroom caps

1 red pepper cut into half lengthwise

1 small red onion, sliced thinly

1 small tomato, sliced thinly

1/2 cup feta or 4 thick slices of Swiss or the equivalent

Prepare grill. Whisk together olive oil, balsamic vinegar, minced garlic, parsley, mustard and salt and pepper. Take a fork and poke holes in the eggplant, zucchini, mushroom caps and red peppers. Using half of the mixture, marinate the eggplant, zucchini, mushroom caps and red peppers for at least an hour. Brush remaining half of mixture on insides of bread and put top and bottom together. Grill marinated vegetables for 10-12 minutes on each side or until golden brown and the red pepper is blackened. Assemble sandwich in the following order, working from the bottom: eggplant, half the cheese, zucchini, mushroom caps, red pepper, onion, tomato and remaining cheese.

Close sandwich and press down firmly for about 30 seconds. Slice into wedges and serve. Serves approximately four.

            *   *   *

Spinach and Lemon Pizza on a Cornbread Crust with Walnuts, Chicken and Rosemary

I developed this yummy treat to use spinach and rosemary from the garden.

2 boxes or bags cornbread mix

One egg

Milk

1/2 cup flour

1 large bunch of spinach, coarsely chopped

3 tbsp. olive oil

1 lemon, cut in half

Salt and pepper

1/2 cup prepared or homemade tomato sauce

2 skinless chicken breasts, cut into 1/2 inch pieces

1 small onion, thinly sliced

1 1/2 cups mozzarella cheese, grated

1/2 cup walnuts, chopped

2 tbsp. fresh or dried rosemary

1/3 cup parmesan cheese

Preheat oven to 400°. Mix cornbread packages, egg, 1/2 cup flour with enough milk to make a consistency that's easy to spread, like a soft cookie dough. Grease a round pizza pan and spread crust on pan, forming a small ridge around the edge. Pre-bake crust for five minutes and set aside. Heat olive oil on medium high in a large skillet. Add spinach and cover to wilt for about one minute. Place spinach in strainer and with the back of a spoon, press out excess moisture. Squeeze the juice of half the lemon on spinach and toss. Sauté chicken and onions on medium high in two tbsps. oil for approximately ten minutes or until chicken is cooked through. Spread spaghetti sauce on crust to cover entire crust. Spread spinach over sauce and place chicken and onions on spinach. Sprinkle grated cheese and walnuts on top and place in oven for 15-17 minutes or until cheese browns. Remove pizza and sprinkle with rosemary and Parmesan cheese. Squeeze other half of lemon over pizza and serve.

*   *   *

Rye Crisp Pizza

This is my favorite meal from my first diet when I was ten. The pizzas are actually very good and easy.

2 whole Rye Crisp crackers (as they come packaged)

1/2 pound ground beef

1 small onion, sliced

1/2 cup tomato sauce

2 tbsp. chopped basil

1 tsp. oregano

Salt and pepper to taste

1/2 cup mushrooms, sliced

6 thin slices of green pepper

1/4 cup green olives, sliced

1 cup mozzarella cheese, grated

Preheat oven to 400°. Cook ground beef and onion in a skillet on medium high heat until cooked through, stirring often. Drain the fat from the skillet and add tomato sauce, basil, oregano, salt, pepper and mushrooms and stir. Spread mixture evenly over the two crackers. Top with green peppers, olives and cheese. Bake for 12 minutes or until cheese has browned. Serves two.

*   *   *

Roast Chicken with Garlic and Herbs

Roasting Chicken

   1 tbsp. fresh or dried rosemary, finely minced

   1 tbsp. sage, ground

   1 tbsp. thyme, ground

   10 garlic cloves, peeled and minced

   4 tbsp. olive oil

   Salt and pepper to taste

   1 whole lemon

Preheat oven to 400°. After washing the chicken in cool water, pat dry and loosen the skin of breasts and thighs by gently sliding your hand under. In a small bowl or covered jar, mix or shake the herbs, garlic, 3 tbsp. of olive oil and salt and pepper. Spread the mixture evenly under the skin, and over the breasts and thigh areas of the bird. Spread the additional tbsp. of olive oil over the outer skin. Using a fork, poke numerous holes over the surface of the lemon and insert into the cavity of the chicken. Tie legs together with a 6 inch piece of string. Place chicken, breast side up in a roasting pan, preferably with a roasting rack in the bottom of the pan to prevent the bird from cooking in the fat drippings, or place on a chicken cone. Cover the pan with aluminum foil and bake for 60 minutes. Raise temperature to 425°, uncover the chicken and bake for an additional 20-30 minutes or until the skin is browned and the juices run clear when a fork is stuck in a breast. Remove from oven and allow to set for ten minutes before serving. Serves four. Goes great with garlic mashed potatoes.

*   *   *

Crystal Light Chicken

This is an easy, fun little dish and very tasty. Goes well with curried vegetables, asparagus and mashed potatoes

2 cups prepared Crystal Light lemonade drink

2 skinless, boneless chicken breasts, thawed

1 cup fat-free half and half

1/4 cup parsley, chopped

1 small red pepper, chopped

Salt and pepper to taste

In a large skillet, bring the Crystal Light to boil. Add chicken and reduce to medium. Cook for 5 minutes, turn chicken and add red pepper. Cook for another five minutes or until chicken is done (juices run clear when a fork is inserted). Reduce to medium and add half and half, parsley, salt and pepper. Allow to cook until sauce thickens, about five minutes. Serve breasts on a plate with sauce poured over them. Serves two.

*   *   *

Just Desserts

Rhubarb & Pineapple Bread Pudding

We need to keep the rhubarb tradition alive. I love how the familiar ruffled mounds dot the backyards of any neighborhood older than 30 years. Rhubarb was such a staple of a time gone by—very accessible, but very versatile. By the end of summer, your stalks may be a little old and a little tough, especially if you have ignored the plant over the summer, but this recipe will soften even the hardest stems. Serve it warm, right out of the oven. It's best with Cool Whip. It's also a relatively low-fat treat.

4 cups rhubarb, cut into 1/2 pieces

1/3 cup sugar

Small can (5 1/2 oz.) crushed pineapple in it's own juice, or 3/4 cup fresh

1 cup chopped walnuts

1/2 cup packed brown sugar

4 cups cubed bread (white or light wheat)

2 large eggs

2 cups skim or 1% milk

1/4 cup white sugar

Pinch of salt

1 tbsp. vanilla extract

1/4 cup light rum (optional)

Preheat oven to 350°. Butter or spray a 9 by 13 inch cake pan with non-stick spray. Combine rhubarb with a 1/2 cup of sugar in a large bowl. Add pineapple and juice, 1/2 cup of the walnuts and brown sugar. Spread the combined mixture over the bottom of the pan. Cover with the cubed bread. Beat together the eggs, milk, white sugar, salt, vanilla and rum (optional) with a whisk until slightly frothy. Pour over the bread. Bake for 50 minutes or until lightly browned on top. Best served warm with ice cream or Cool Whip.

*   *   *

Lemon Zucchini Gingerbread

If you grow zucchini, you know the productivity potential. If the squash borer bug doesn't get your plant, the zucchini will deliver until frost. I love sliced zucchini best when it is simply sautéed with a sliced onion in a dab of olive oil and then sprinkled with curry powder (a simple and light side dish). The truth of the matter is every gardener needs a good device for getting rid of the prolific devils. Along comes zucchini bread. The following bread is easy (it uses a store-bought mix), tangy (from the lemon) and uses up two medium fruits. It is fabulous as a dessert or for breakfast or brunch.

1 store bought gingerbread mix

2 medium or 4 small zucchini, finely minced by hand or in a processor

1 egg

1 large lemonade concentrate

Preheat oven to 350°. In a large bowl, combine mix, zucchini and egg (eliminate water from the mix). Pour into a lightly greased ten by four inch bread plan. Bake for 45 minutes or until the top of loaf springs back when pressed. Allow to cool. Bring lemonade to a boil in a small saucepan. Reduce and simmer for 10 minutes to reduce mixture. With a skewer, poke many holes in the gingerbread, all over. Slowly pour reduced concentrate over bread and allow to set for half an hour. Serve with a sliver of lemon peel on top.

*   *   *

A Vegetable Cookie? Lime Cilantro Puckers

Cilantro is such a light and distinctive herb. These cookies are clearly flecked with green, but are very sweet and zingy. They go well with a cold beer on a lazy afternoon in the garden, if you are so inclined.

1 cup powdered sugar

1 cup white sugar

1 cup vegetable shortening

1 beaten egg

1 tsp. vanilla

1 tsp. salt

1 tsp. baking powder

1 tsp. cream of tartar

3 tbsp. minced cilantro

3 cups flour (or enough to make consistency of Play-Doh)

Rind and pulp of 1 lime, very finely minced in a food processor

White sugar

Cilantro leaves

Preheat oven to 350°. Cream sugars, shortening, eggs and vanilla. Stir in remaining ingredients. Form into balls the size of cherry tomatoes, roll in white sugar and place on a lightly greased cookie sheet, 2 inches apart. Flatten balls with the bottom of a drinking glass. Gently place a cilantro leaf or piece of a leaf on each cookie. Bake for 15 minutes in the center of the oven. Cool. Makes approximately 50.

             *   *   *

If you eat only one more chocolate chip cookie in your life...

Make it this one. It is the absolute best...no contest.

3/4 cups butter

1 cup sugar

1 cup brown sugar

2 eggs

1/2 tsp. vanilla

2 cups flour

2 1/2 cups oatmeal

1/4 tsp. salt

1 tsp. soda

1 tsp. baking powder

12 oz. chocolate chips

4 oz. chocolate bar, grated

1/3 cup chopped walnuts

Preheat oven to 350°. Cream together butter and sugars in a large bowl. Add beaten eggs and vanilla. In a separate bowl, mix the flour, oatmeal, salt, soda and baking powder. Mix dry ingredients into wet ingredients. Add the chocolates and nuts. Bake on a non-greased cookie sheet for 12 minutes or until golden.

Afterword

I rebelled a bit while writing this book. It was as if something inside me had to test everything that I was putting down on paper. Even though I was writing that skipping meals was the surest way to drive yourself to overeat, I occasionally did it. Even though I was documenting the powers of eating protein at every meal, sometimes I didn't. And even though I was touting that you are okay exactly as you are, there were times when I didn't think I was.

Losing weight is not about being perfect. Things are going to come up along the way that will get you off track. The secret to weight loss is getting back on track as quickly as you can. This is probably the most crucial of any of the ideas I've presented to you. When I was in my full-blown days of dieting and the good/bad food mindset, I would wake up every morning, vowing that this was the first day of the rest of my perfect eating life. Nothing bad would ever enter my mouth, and I would eat only perfect portions. Who could live up to that? Talk about setting yourself up for failure! And talk about a boring way to live!

Find your joy in life. Living is not about dividing food into palm-sized portions and hoping for the scale to tell you tomorrow morning that you are good. Do what makes you really happy. Discover your passions. Look for activities, hobbies and work that ignite a rumble of excitement in your belly. Get involved in your life. Losing weight may have developed into one of the few things you spend your time thinking about. That's okay…it proves how important it is to you. But if you cultivate all of the many other wonderful things that make up you, they will help you uncover your true self, find real happiness and true joy, and quite simply, keep your mind off of food.

That isn't to say that your new way of eating and exercising isn't going to consume you for a while. It will, and that is good. A little initial obsession goes a long way. Habits, even healthy ones, take a while to settle into our psyches. Plan your meals, schedule your exercise, bring baggies of your favorite, healthy foods where you go, read books and magazine articles on weight loss, tape photos of success stories on your refrigerator, write in a journal as often as you need. Feel free to be a little obsessed, especially at the beginning. But, make sure you are also obsessed about bringing into your life that which makes your spirit soar…your favorite pastimes, foods, exercises, and even work.

*   *   *

I understand how you want to lose weight so badly it makes your heart ache and consumes your every thought. I know how badly you want to have a peaceful relationship with food. I realize that you want to be happy. Being thin will not make you instantly happy. But, the process to getting thin will sure help. You learn to trust yourself when you lose weight. After a few instances of passing up Cheetos in the afternoon (which were never your favorite snack food anyway) and avoiding cleaning up dinner at 10 p.m. as you stand at the open fridge, you will begin to get in touch with how you really want to eat. You soon learn that you really do have the final say over what goes into your mouth and, ultimately, what your body looks like. And when you discover that you really do have the right to eat your favorite foods and to have something good to eat every couple of hours, eating is no longer torture. You are so full of possibilities. You can have anything you wish.

Why don't you start this very moment?

Bibliography

Dyer, Wayne W. *Manifest Your Destiny*. New York: Harper Collins, 1997.

Editors of Prevention Magazine. *Natural Weight Loss*. Emmaus: Rodale Press, 1985.

Gawain, Shakti. *Creative Visualization*. San Rafael: Bantam, 1983.

Gray, John. *How to Get What You Want and Want What You Have: A Practical and Spiritual Guide to Personal Success*. New York: Harper Collins, 2000.

Heller, Drs. Richard F and Rachel F. *The Carbohydrate Addict's Lifespan Program*. New York: Penguin Books, 1998.

McGee, Harold. *On Food and Cooking, The Science and Lore of the Kitchen*. New York: Simon & Schuster, 1984.

Phillips, Bill. *Body for Life*. New York: Harper Collins, 1999.

Robertson, Laurel, Flinders, Carol, and Godfrey, Bronwen. *Laurel's Kitchen*. Petaluma: Nilgiri Press, 1978.

Ruiz, Don Miguel. *The Four Agreements: A Practical Guide to Personal Freedom*. San Rafael: Amber-Allen, 1997.

Zukav, Gary. *Seat of the Soul*. New York: Fireside, 1990.

Zukav, Gary. *Soul Stories*. New York: Simon & Schuster, 2000.

About the Author

Eric Johnson is a professional actor and published writer who lives in South Minneapolis. He is also a graphic designer, potter, painter, and passionate cook and gardener. Weight problems and overeating run in his family, but so do creativity, love, patience, good humor, and optimism.